Flinn Scientific
ChemTopic™ Labs

Chemical Bonding

Senior Editor

Irene Cesa
Flinn Scientific, Inc.
Batavia, IL

Curriculum Advisory Board

Bob Becker
Kirkwood High School
Kirkwood, MO

Kathleen J. Dombrink
McCluer North High School
Florissant, MO

Robert Lewis
Downers Grove North High School
Downers Grove, IL

John G. Little
St. Mary's High School
Stockton, CA

Lee Marek
University of Illinois–Chicago
Chicago, IL

John Mauch
Braintree High School
Braintree, MA

Dave Tanis
Grand Valley State University
Allendale, MI

FLINN SCIENTIFIC INC.
"Your Safer Source for Science Supplies"
P.O. Box 219 • Batavia, IL 60510
1-800-452-1261 • www.flinnsci.com

ISBN 1-877991-73-2

Copyright © 2004 Flinn Scientific, Inc.

All rights reserved. No part of this book may be reproduced or transmitted in any form or by any means, electronic or mechanical, including, but not limited to photocopy, recording, or any information storage and retrieval system, without permission in writing from Flinn Scientific, Inc.
No part of this book may be included on any Web site.

Reproduction permission is granted only to the science teacher who has purchased this volume of Flinn ChemTopic™ Labs, Chemical Bonding, Catalog No. AP6595 from Flinn Scientific, Inc. Science teachers may make copies of the reproducible student pages for use only by their students.

Printed in the United States of America.

Table of Contents

	Page
Flinn ChemTopic™ Labs Series Preface	i
About the Curriculum Advisory Board	ii
Chemical Bonding Preface	iii
Format and Features	iv–v
Experiment Summaries and Concepts	vi–vii

Experiments

Properties of Solids	1
Formula of an Ionic Compound	15
Lewis Structures and Molecular Geometry	27
The Color of Chemistry	45

Demonstrations

Go Fish for an Ion	61
Electronegativity	65
Splatter Test	67
Graphite Disk Demonstration	69
Properties of Metals	71
Super Duper Polymer	75

Supplementary Information

Safety and Disposal Guidelines	78
National Science Education Standards	80
Master Materials Guide	82

Flinn ChemTopic™ Labs — Chemical Bonding

Flinn ChemTopic™ Labs Series Preface
Lab Manuals Organized Around Key Content Areas in Chemistry

In conversations with chemistry teachers across the country, we have heard a common concern. Teachers are frustrated with their current lab manuals, with experiments that are poorly designed and don't teach core concepts, with procedures that are rigid and inflexible and don't work. Teachers want greater flexibility in their choice of lab activities. As we further listened to experienced master teachers who regularly lead workshops and training seminars, another theme emerged. Master teachers mostly rely on collections of experiments and demonstrations they have put together themselves over the years. Some activities have been passed on like cherished family recipe cards from one teacher to another. Others have been adapted from one format to another to take advantage of new trends in microscale equipment and procedures, technology innovations, and discovery-based learning theory. In all cases the experiments and demonstrations have been fine-tuned based on real classroom experience.

Flinn Scientific has developed a series of lab manuals based on these "cherished recipe cards" of master teachers with proven excellence in both teaching students and training teachers. Created under the direction of an Advisory Board of award-winning chemistry teachers, each lab manual in the Flinn ChemTopic™ Labs series contains 4–6 student-tested experiments that focus on essential concepts and applications in a single content area. Each lab manual also contains 4–6 demonstrations that can be used to illustrate a chemical property, reaction or relationship and will capture your students' attention. The experiments and demonstrations in the Flinn ChemTopic™ Labs series are enjoyable, highly focused, and will give students a real sense of accomplishment.

Laboratory experiments allow students to experience chemistry by doing chemistry. Experiments have been selected to provide students with a crystal-clear understanding of chemistry concepts and encourage students to think about these concepts critically and analytically. Well-written procedures are guaranteed to work. Reproducible data tables teach students how to organize their data so it is easily analyzed. Comprehensive teacher notes include a master materials list, solution preparation guide, complete sample data, and answers to all questions. Detailed lab hints and teaching tips show you how to conduct the experiment in your lab setting and how to identify student errors and misconceptions before students are led astray.

Chemical demonstrations provide another teaching tool for seeing chemistry in action. Because they are both visual and interactive, demonstrations allow teachers to take students on a journey of observation and understanding. Demonstrations provide additional resources to develop central themes and to magnify the power of observation in the classroom. Demonstrations using discrepant events challenge student misconceptions that must be broken down before new concepts can be learned. Use demonstrations to introduce new ideas, illustrate abstract concepts that cannot be covered in lab experiments, and provide a spark of excitement that will capture student interest and attention.

Safety, flexibility, and choice

Safety always comes first. Depend on Flinn Scientific to give you upfront advice and guidance on all safety and disposal issues. Each activity begins with a description of the hazards involved and the necessary safety precautions to avoid exposure to these hazards. Additional safety, handling, and disposal information is also contained in the teacher notes.

The selection of experiments and demonstrations in each Flinn ChemTopic™ Labs manual gives you the flexibility to choose activities that match the concepts your students need to learn. No single teacher will do all of the experiments and demonstrations with a single class. Some experiments and demonstrations may be more helpful with a beginning-level class, while others may be more suitable with an honors class. All of the experiments and demonstrations have been keyed to national content standards in science education.

Chemistry is an experimental science!

Whether they are practicing key measurement skills or searching for trends in the chemical properties of substances, all students will benefit from the opportunity to discover chemistry by doing chemistry. No matter what chemistry textbook you use in the classroom, Flinn ChemTopic™ Labs will help you give your students the necessary knowledge, skills, attitudes, and values to be successful in chemistry.

About the Curriculum Advisory Board

Flinn Scientific is honored to work with an outstanding group of dedicated chemistry teachers. The members of the Flinn ChemTopic Labs Advisory Board have generously contributed their proven experiments and demonstrations to create these topic lab manuals. The wisdom, experience, creativity, and insight reflected in their lab activities guarantee that students who perform them will be more successful in learning chemistry. On behalf of all chemistry teachers, we thank the Advisory Board members for their service and dedication to chemistry education.

Bob Becker teaches chemistry and AP chemistry at Kirkwood High School in Kirkwood, MO. Bob received his B.A. from Yale University and M.Ed. from Washington University and has 20 years of teaching experience. A well-known demonstrator, Bob has conducted more than 100 demonstration workshops across the U.S. and Canada and was a Team Leader for the Flinn Foundation Summer Workshop Program. His creative and unusual demonstrations have been published in the *Journal of Chemical Education,* the *Science Teacher,* and *Chem13 News.* Bob is the author of two books of chemical demonstrations, *Twenty Demonstrations Guaranteed to Knock Your Socks Off, Volumes I and II,* published by Flinn Scientific. Bob has been awarded the James Bryant Conant Award in High School Teaching from the American Chemical Society, the Regional Catalyst Award from the Chemical Manufacturers Association, and the Tandy Technology Scholar Award.

Kathleen J. Dombrink teaches chemistry and advanced-credit college chemistry at McCluer North High School in Florissant, MO. Kathleen received her B.A. in Chemistry from Holy Names College and M.S. in Chemistry from St. Louis University and has 35 years of teaching experience. Recognized for her strong support of professional development, Kathleen has been selected to participate in the Fulbright Memorial Fund Teacher Program in Japan and NEWMAST and Dow/NSTA Workshops. She served as co-editor of the inaugural issues of *Chem Matters* and was a Woodrow Wilson National Fellowship Foundation Chemistry Team Member for 11 years. Kathleen is currently a Team Leader for the Flinn Foundation Summer Workshop Program. Kathleen has received the Presidential Award, the Midwest Regional Teaching Award from the American Chemical Society, the Tandy Technology Scholar Award, and a Regional Catalyst Award from the Chemical Manufacturers Association.

Robert Lewis recently retired from teaching chemistry at Downers Grove North High School in Downers Grove, IL, and is currently a Secondary Coordinator for the GATE program in Chicago. Robert received his B.A. from North Central College and M.A. from University of the South and has 30 years of teaching experience. He was a founding member of Weird Science, a group of chemistry teachers that traveled throughout the country to stimulate teacher enthusiasm for using demonstrations to teach science. Robert served as a Team Leader for both the Woodrow Wilson National Fellowship Foundation and the Flinn Foundation Summer Workshop Program. Robert has received the Presidential Award, the James Bryant Conant Award in High School Teaching from the American Chemical Society, the Tandy Technology Scholar Award, a Regional Catalyst Award from the Chemical Manufacturers Association, and a Golden Apple Award from the State of Illinois.

John G. Little teaches chemistry and AP chemistry at St. Mary's High School in Stockton, CA. John received his B.S. and M.S. in Chemistry from University of the Pacific and has 39 years of teaching experience. Highly respected for his well-designed labs, John is the author of two lab manuals, *Chemistry Microscale Laboratory Manual* (D. C. Heath), and *Microscale Experiments for General Chemistry* (with Kenneth Williamson, Houghton Mifflin). He is also a contributing author to *Science Explorer* (Prentice Hall) and *World of Chemistry* (McDougal Littell). John served as a Chemistry Team Leader for both the Woodrow Wilson National Fellowship Foundation and the Flinn Foundation Summer Workshop Program. He has been recognized for his dedicated teaching with the Tandy Technology Scholar Award and the Regional Catalyst Award from the Chemical Manufacturers Association.

Lee Marek retired from teaching chemistry at Naperville North High School in Naperville, IL and currently teaches at the University of Illinois–Chicago. Lee received his B.S. in Chemical Engineering from the University of Illinois and M.S. degrees in both Physics and Chemistry from Roosevelt University. He has more than 30 years of teaching experience and is currently a Team Leader for the Flinn Foundation Summer Workshop Program. His students have won national recognition in the International Chemistry Olympiad, the Westinghouse Science Talent Search, and the Internet Science and Technology Fair. Lee was also a founding member of Weird Science and has presented more than 500 demonstration and teaching workshops for more than 300,000 students and teachers across the country. Lee has performed science demonstrations on the *David Letterman Show* 20 times. Lee has received the Presidential Award, the James Bryant Conant Award in High School Teaching and the Helen M. Free Award for Public Outreach from the American Chemical Society, the National Catalyst Award from the Chemical Manufacturers Association, and the Tandy Technology Scholar Award.

John Mauch teaches chemistry and AP chemistry at Braintree High School in Braintree, MA. John received his B.A. in Chemistry from Whitworth College and M.A. in Curriculum and Education from Washington State University and has more than 25 years of teaching experience. John is an expert in microscale chemistry and is the author of two lab manuals, *Chemistry in Microscale, Volumes I and II* (Kendall/Hunt). He is also a dynamic and prolific demonstrator and workshop leader. John has presented the Flinn Scientific Chem Demo Extravaganza show at NSTA conventions for eight years and has conducted more than 100 workshops across the country. John was a Chemistry Team Member for the Woodrow Wilson National Fellowship Foundation program and is currently a Board Member for the Flinn Foundation Summer Workshop Program. John has received the Massachusetts Chemistry Teacher of the Year Award from the New England Institute of Chemists.

Dave Tanis is Associate Professor of Chemistry at Grand Valley State University in Allendale, MI. Dave received his B.S. in Physics and Mathematics from Calvin College and M.S. in Chemistry from Case Western Reserve University. He taught high school chemistry for 26 years before joining the staff at Grand Valley State University to direct a coalition for improving pre-college math and science education. Dave later joined the faculty at Grand Valley State University and currently teaches courses for pre-service teachers. The author of two laboratory manuals, Dave acknowledges the influence of early encounters with Hubert Alyea, Marge Gardner, Henry Heikkinen, and Bassam Shakhashiri in stimulating his long-standing interest in chemical demonstrations and experiments. Continuing this tradition of mentorship, Dave has led more than 40 one-week institutes for chemistry teachers and served as a Team Member for the Woodrow Wilson National Fellowship Foundation for 13 years. He is currently a Board Member for the Flinn Foundation Summer Workshop Program. Dave received the College Science Teacher of the Year Award from the Michigan Science Teachers Association.

Preface
Chemical Bonding

Chemical bonding describes interactions among atoms. What kinds of forces hold atoms together in a molecule or compound? How does the nature of the forces holding atoms together influence the properties of a material? Looking for patterns in the properties of solids and liquids can help us see inside the hidden world of atoms and molecules, to visualize and describe the forces holding atoms together. The purpose of *Chemical Bonding*, Volume 5 in the Flinn ChemTopic™ Labs series, is to provide high school chemistry teachers with laboratory activities that will help students understand how theories of chemical bonding have developed to explain and predict the properties of materials. Four experiments and six demonstrations allow students to investigate ionic, covalent, and metallic bonding and to explore the relationships between the properties of a material, its structure, and chemical bonding.

Structure and Bonding

Chemical bonding provides a conceptual framework to explain the properties of materials. Students investigate the behavior of common solids with a wide range of physical properties in "Properties of Solids," an introductory experiment which serves as an overview of ionic, covalent, and metallic bonding. Which solids will conduct electricity? Which solids will dissolve in water? What differences in bonding and structure will explain why some solids are hard and brittle while others are hard and nonbrittle? Models of crystal structure can help students visualize the nature of bonding interactions in solids. Structure and bonding are formally combined in "Properties of Metals," a unique activity in which students observe the changes brought about by the heat treatment of metals and then examine models of crystal structure to explain the changes.

Ionic and Covalent Bonding

Determining the formulas of ionic and covalent compounds is a challenge for many students. In "Formula of an Ionic Compound," students carry out a series of microscale precipitation reactions by mixing solutions in different ratios. The amount of precipitate is measured and plotted against the volume ratio of reactants to find the empirical formula of the unknown ionic product. The "Go Fish for an Ion" card game provides a fun way for students to review the formulas of ionic compounds prior to a test. Although learning the rules of ionic compound formation requires lots of practice and review, the rules of covalent bond formation often seem downright baffling to students. Why does carbon form both carbon monoxide and carbon dioxide? What is the difference between phosphorus trichloride and phosphorus pentachloride? The reasons for the rules begin to make sense in "Lewis Structures and Molecular Geometry." In this dry-lab activity, students practice drawing Lewis structures for molecules and learn why atoms need to form a certain number of bonds in order to form stable molecules. Students then work with molecular models in order to predict the three-dimensional structures and shapes of molecules.

Bonding and Intermolecular Forces

Forces between molecules arise due to differences in the bonding between atoms. Both chemical bonding and intermolecular forces play an important role in "The Color of Chemistry." In this applications-oriented experiment, students investigate the interaction of a variety of dyes with a special multifiber fabric. The brilliant and intriguing color patterns produced by different dyes on different fabrics teach students about the chemical structures of dye and fabric molecules and the bonding interactions between them. The influence of intermolecular forces on the properties of molecules is also on display in the "Splatter Test," "Graphite Disk," and "Super Duper Polymer" demonstrations.

Learning in the Lab

Chemistry is an experimental science! Depend on Flinn Scientific to give you the information and confidence you need to work safely with your students and help them succeed. As your safer source for science supplies, Flinn Scientific promises you the most complete, reliable, and practical safety information for every potential lab hazard. The selection of experiments and demonstrations in *Chemical Bonding*—combined with complete sample data and extensive teacher notes—gives you the ability to design an effective lab curriculum that will work with your students and your resources in your classroom. Best of all, no matter which activities you choose, your students are assured of success. All of the activities in *Chemical Bonding* have been thoroughly tested and retested. You know they will work! Use the experiment summaries and concepts on the following pages to locate the concepts you want to teach and to choose experiments and demonstrations that will help you meet your goals.

Format and Features

Flinn ChemTopic™ Labs

All experiments and demonstrations in Flinn ChemTopic™ Labs are printed in a 10⅞" × 11" format with a wide 2" margin on the inside of each page. This reduces the printed area of each page to a standard 8½" × 11" format suitable for copying.

The wide margin assures you the entire printed area can be easily reproduced without damaging the binding. The margin also provides a convenient place for teachers to add their own notes.

Concepts — Use these bulleted lists along with state and local standards, lesson plans, and your textbook to identify activities that will allow you to accomplish specific learning goals and objectives.

Background — A balanced source of information for students to understand why they are doing an experiment, what they are doing, and the types of questions the activity is designed to answer. This section is not meant to be exhaustive or to replace the students' textbook, but rather to identify the core concepts that should be covered before starting the lab.

Experiment Overview — Clearly defines the purpose of each experiment and how students will achieve this goal. Performing an experiment without a purpose is like getting travel directions without knowing your destination. It doesn't work, especially if you run into a roadblock and need to take a detour!

Pre-Lab Questions — Making sure that students are prepared for lab is the single most important element of lab safety. Pre-lab questions introduce new ideas or concepts, review key calculations, and reinforce safety recommendations. The pre-lab questions may be assigned as homework in preparation for lab or they may be used as the basis of a cooperative class activity before lab.

Materials — Lists chemical names, formulas, and amounts for all reagents—along with specific glassware and equipment—needed to perform the experiment as written. The material dispensing area is a main source of student delay, congestion, and accidents. Three dispensing stations per room are optimum for a class of 24 students working in pairs. To safely substitute different items for any of the recommended materials, refer to the *Lab Hints* section in each experiment or demonstration.

Safety Precautions — Instruct and warn students of the hazards associated with the materials or procedure and give specific recommendations and precautions to protect students from these hazards. Please review this section with students before beginning each experiment.

Procedure — This section contains a stepwise, easy-to-follow procedure, where each step generally refers to one action item. Contains reminders about safety and recording data where appropriate. For inquiry-based experiments the procedure may restate the experiment objective and give general guidelines for accomplishing this goal.

Data Tables — Data tables are included for each experiment and are referred to in the procedure. These are provided for convenience and to teach students the importance of keeping their data organized in order to analyze it. To encourage more student involvement, many teachers prefer to have students prepare their own data tables. This is an excellent pre-lab preparation activity—it ensures that students have read the procedure and are prepared for lab.

Post-Lab Questions or Data Analysis — This section takes students step-by-step through what they did, what they observed, and what it means. Meaningful questions encourage analysis and promote critical thinking skills. Where students need to perform calculations or graph data to analyze the results, these steps are also laid out sequentially for students to follow.

Format and Features

Teacher's Notes

Master Materials List Lists the chemicals, glassware, and equipment needed to perform the experiment. All amounts have been calculated for a class of 30 students working in pairs. For smaller or larger class sizes or different working group sizes, please adjust the amounts proportionately.

Preparation of Solutions Calculations and procedures are given for preparing all solutions, based on a class size of 30 students working in pairs. With the exception of particularly hazardous materials, the solution amounts generally include 10% extra to account for spillage and waste. Solution volumes may be rounded to convenient glassware sizes (100-mL, 250-mL, 500-mL, etc.).

Safety Precautions Repeats the safety precautions given to the students and includes more detailed information relating to safety and handling of chemicals and glassware. Refers to Material Safety Data Sheets that should be available for all chemicals used in the laboratory.

Disposal Refers to the current *Flinn Scientific Catalog/Reference Manual* for general guidelines and specific procedures governing the disposal of laboratory waste. Because we recommend that teachers review local regulations before beginning any disposal procedure, the information given in this section is for general reference purposes only. However, if a disposal step is included as part of the experimental procedure itself, then the specific solutions needed for disposal are described in this section.

Lab Hints This section reveals common sources of student errors and misconceptions and where students are likely to need help. Identifies the recommended length of time needed to perform each experiment, suggests alternative chemicals and equipment that may be used, and reminds teachers about new techniques (filtration, pipeting, etc.) that should be reviewed prior to lab.

Teaching Tips This section puts the experiment in perspective so that teachers can judge in more detail how and where a particular experiment will fit into their curriculum. Identifies the working assumptions about what students need to know in order to perform the experiment and answer the questions. Highlights historical background and applications-oriented information that may be of interest to students.

Sample Data Complete, actual sample data obtained by performing the experiment exactly as written is included for each experiment. Student data will vary.

Answers to All Questions Representative or typical answers to all questions. Includes sample calculations and graphs for all data analysis questions. Information of special interest to teachers only in this section is identified by the heading "Note to the teacher." Student answers will vary.

Look for these icons in the *Experiment Summaries and Concepts* section and in the *Teacher's Notes* of individual experiments to identify inquiry-, microscale-, and technology-based experiments, respectively.

Experiment Summaries and Concepts

Experiment

Properties of Solids—Structure and Bonding

Looking for patterns in the properties of different substances can help students understand how and why atoms join together to form compounds. What kinds of forces hold atoms together? How does the nature of the forces holding atoms together influence the properties of a material? The purpose of this experiment is to study the physical properties of common solids and to investigate the relationship between the type of bonding in a substance and its properties.

Formula of an Ionic Compound—Balancing Charges on Ions

Atoms of different elements combine with one another to form compounds. The empirical formula of an ionic compound indicates the kinds of atoms that are present in the compound and their relative ratio. The purpose of this microscale experiment is to determine the empirical formula of an unknown ionic compound. Students carry out a series of precipitation reactions by mixing two solutions in different ratios. The amount of precipitate obtained in each reaction is measured and plotted against the volume ratio of reactants to find the empirical formula of the product.

Lewis Structures and Molecular Geometry—Models of Covalent Bonding

Molecules have shape! The structure and shape of a molecule influences its physical properties and affects its chemical behavior as well. The purpose of this activity is to practice drawing Lewis structures of molecules and examine molecular models to visualize the three-dimensional structures of molecules. Words and pictures on a printed page are no substitute for models that students can hold in their hands, rotate, turn upside down, even take apart and put back together again. Students develop the spatial reasoning skills required for success in chemistry as they discover how atoms join together to make molecules.

The Color of Chemistry—Dyes, Dyeing, and Chemical Bonding

What is your favorite color? Color affects our senses, our moods, even our learning. In this experiment, students investigate the interaction of a variety of dyes with a special multifiber test fabric containing strips of wool, acrylic, polyester, nylon, cotton, and acetate. The brilliant color patterns produced by different dyes teach students about the chemical structures of dye and fabric molecules and the types of bonding interactions between them.

Concepts

- Chemical bonds
- Ionic bonding
- Covalent bonding
- Metallic bonding

- Ionic compounds
- Empirical formula
- Polyatomic ions
- Precipitation reaction

- Valence electrons
- Covalent bonding
- Lewis structures
- VSEPR theory

- Chemical bonding
- Ionic bonds
- Polar vs. nonpolar bonds
- Hydrogen bonding

Experiment Summaries and Concepts

Demonstration

Concepts

Go Fish for an Ion—A Chemistry Card Game

"Go fish!" in the fishing pond of ion cards! Have fun while reviewing the names and charges of common ions and the formulas of ionic compounds with this engaging chemistry card game. All students are actively involved as they form compounds using ion cards for 20 different cations and anions, review matches made by other players, and keep detailed score sheets. Completed score sheets make perfect study guides when it's time to prepare for the test.

- Ionic compounds
- Empirical formulas
- Cations and anions
- Ion charges

Electronegativity—A Simple Demonstration Device

Teachers at all levels appreciate the effectiveness of concrete models to teach students about abstract concepts. Help students visualize the origin and nature of electronegativity using this inexpensive and easy-to-make demonstration device. Rubber bands and Styrofoam® spheres demonstrate the tug-of-war between atoms for the bonding pair of electrons in nonpolar and polar covalent bonds.

- Covalent bonding
- Nonpolar vs. polar bonds
- Electronegativity
- Bonding electron pair

Splatter Test—Properties of Liquids Demonstration

The properties of liquids reflect the bonding within molecules and the nature and strength of forces between molecules. The "Splatter Test" demonstration will leave your students with a lasting impression of how intermolecular forces between molecules affect the rate of evaporation of a liquid.

- Intermolecular forces
- Hydrogen bonding
- Dipole–dipole interactions

Graphite Disk Demonstration—Face-up or Face-down?

Paper and graphite (pencil lead) have very different properties. Place graphite-coated paper disks in two-phase solvent systems containing water and a nonpolar organic solvent and observe the orientation of the disks—face-up or face-down? Will it be random? Always up or always down? Find out with this unique demonstration.

- Covalent bonds
- Polar vs. nonpolar compounds
- Density

Properties of Metals—Crystal Structure and Heat Treatment

Heat treatment of metals is used to increase their hardness and improve their "workability"—their ability to be bent and shaped. Annealing, hardening, and tempering produce remarkable changes in the properties of metals. Discover the effects of heating and cooling metals and correlate the changes with models of crystal structure with this interesting "bobby pin" activity.

- Properties of metals
- Crystal structure
- Body-centered cubic
- Face-centered cubic

Super Duper Polymer—Polyethylene Oxide Demonstration

Hydrogen bonding produces gravity-defying special effects in this classic demonstration of the properties of a unique polymer. Principles of bonding and structure become large enough to see if you make the molecules big enough!

- Polymers
- Hydrogen bonding
- Bond lengths and bond angles

Properties of Solids
Structure and Bonding

Teacher Notes

Introduction

Looking for patterns in the properties of different substances can help us understand how and why atoms join together to form compounds. What kinds of forces hold atoms together? How does the nature of the forces holding atoms together influence the properties of a material?

Concepts

- Chemical bonds
- Covalent bonding
- Ionic bonding
- Metallic bonding

Background

Groups of atoms are held together by attractive forces that we call *chemical bonds*. The origin of chemical bonds is reflected in the relationship between force and energy in the physical world. Think about the force of gravity—in order to overcome the force of attraction between an object and the Earth, we have to supply energy. Whether we climb a mountain or throw a ball high into the air, we have to supply energy. Similarly, in order to break a bond between two atoms, energy must be added to the system, usually in the form of heat, light or electricity. The opposite is also true: whenever a bond is formed, energy is released.

The term *ionic bonding* is used to describe the attractive forces between oppositely charged ions in an ionic compound. An ionic compound is formed when a metal reacts with a non-metal to form positively charged cations and negatively charged anions, respectively. The oppositely charged ions arrange themselves in a tightly packed, extended three-dimensional structure called a crystal lattice (see Figure 1). The net attractive forces between oppositely charged ions in the crystal structure are called ionic bonds.

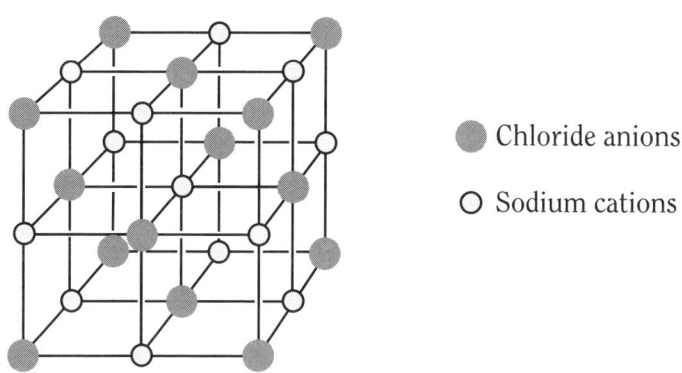

Figure 1. Crystal Structure of Sodium Chloride.

Covalent bonding represents another type of attractive force between atoms. Covalent bonds are defined as the net attractive forces resulting from pairs of electrons that are shared between atoms (the shared electrons are attracted to the nuclei of both atoms in the bond). A group of atoms held together by covalent bonds is called a molecule. Atoms may share one, two or three pairs of electrons between them to form single, double, and triple bonds, respectively.

Many new terms and definitions are introduced in this activity, which provides an overview of all types of chemical bonding. Encourage students to make a list of all the new terminology and write out their definitions. Remind students also to consult their textbooks for additional examples, models, and illustrations that may help explain the concepts.

Substances held together by covalent bonds are usually divided into two groups based on whether individual (distinct) molecules exist or not. In a *molecular solid,* individual molecules in the solid state are attracted to each other by relatively weak intermolecular forces between the molecules. *Covalent-network solids,* on the other hand, consist of atoms forming covalent bonds with each other in all directions. The result is an almost infinite network of strong covalent bonds—there are no individual molecules.

Covalent bonds may be classified as polar or nonpolar. The element chlorine, for example, exists as a diatomic molecule, Cl_2. The two chlorine atoms are held together by a single covalent bond, with the two electrons in the bond equally shared between the two identical chlorine atoms. This type of bond is called a *nonpolar* covalent bond. The compound hydrogen chloride (HCl) consists of a hydrogen atom and a chlorine atom that also share a pair of electrons between them. Because the two atoms are different, however, the electrons in the bond are not equally shared between the atoms. Chlorine has a greater *electronegativity* than hydrogen—it attracts the bonding electrons more strongly than hydrogen. The covalent bond between hydrogen and chlorine is an example of a *polar* bond. The distribution of bonding electrons in a nonpolar versus polar bond is shown in Figure 2. Notice that the chlorine atom in HCl has a partial negative charge (δ^-) while the hydrogen atom has a partial positive charge (δ^+).

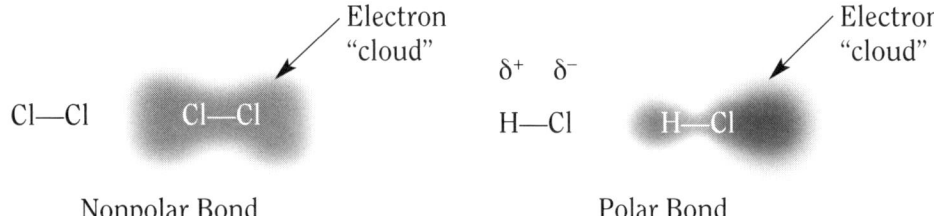

Figure 2. Nonpolar versus Polar Covalent Bonds.

The special properties of metals compared to nonmetals reflect their unique structure and bonding. Metals typically have a small number of valence electrons available for bonding. The valence electrons appear to be free to move among all of the metal atoms, which must exist therefore as positively charged cations. *Metallic bonding* describes the attractive forces that exist between closely packed metal cations and free-floating valence electrons in an extended three-dimensional structure.

Experiment Overview

The purpose of this experiment is to study the physical properties of common solids and to investigate the relationship between the type of bonding in a substance and its properties. The following physical properties will be studied:

- Volatility and Odor: Volatile substances evaporate easily and may have an odor.
- Melting Point: The temperature at which a solid turns into a liquid.
- Solubility: Ability of one substance to dissolve in another. Water is a highly polar solvent. Hexane is nonpolar.
- Conductivity: Ability to conduct electricity.
- Hardness: Resistance of a substance to being scratched.
- Brittleness: Tendency of a solid to break or crumble when a stress is applied.

Teacher Notes

It is hard to convey the principles of bonding and structure using only two-dimensional drawings or pictures. We strongly encourage the use of three-dimensional models to help students recognize and understand the relationship between structure and bonding. Consult your current Flinn Scientific Catalog for a complete selection of models, including diamond (AP6176), graphite (AP6175), ice (AP6178), and sodium chloride (AP6179).

Teacher Notes

Pre-Lab Questions

1. A student wanted to illustrate the structure of magnesium chloride and decided simply to replace the Na⁺ ions in Figure 1 with Mg^{2+} ions. What would be wrong with the resulting picture?

2. Covalent bonds may be classified as polar or nonpolar based on the difference in electronegativity between two atoms. Look up electronegativity values in your textbook:

    (a) Why are C—H bonds considered nonpolar?

    (b) Which is more polar, an O—H or N—H bond?

3. The three dimensional structure of diamond, a crystalline form of the element carbon, is shown in Figure 3. Use this structure to explain why diamond is the hardest known material.

Figure 3.

Materials

Aluminum shot or granules, Al, 0.5 g
Distilled water and wash bottle
Hexane, C_6H_{14}, 5 mL
Silicon dioxide (sand), SiO_2, 0.2–0.3 g
Sodium chloride (salt), NaCl, 0.2–0.3 g
Stearic acid, $C_{18}H_{36}O_2$, 0.2–0.3 g
Sucrose (sugar), $C_{12}H_{22}O_{11}$, 0.2–0.3 g
Minerals for hardness testing (optional)
   Aluminum strip
   Candle (paraffin wax)
   Halite or rock salt (sodium chloride)
   Quartz (silicon dioxide)
   Rock candy (sucrose)
Penny and nail to test hardness (optional)
Balance, centigram
Weighing dishes, 5

Aluminum evaporating dish or Pyrex® watch glass
Beaker, 150-mL
Boiling stones
Bunsen burner*
Conductivity tester, low-voltage*
Hot plate*
Mortars and pestles, 5*
Pipets, Beral-type, 2
Reaction plate, 24-well
Spatula
Stirring rod or toothpicks
Test tubes, Pyrex®, small, 5, or Ceramic spot plate
Test tube rack
Test tube holder (clamp)

*Students may share conductivity testers, hot plates, laboratory burners, and mortars and pestles.

Safety Precautions

Hexane is a flammable organic solvent and a dangerous fire risk. Keep away from flames, heat, and other sources of ignition. Cap the solvent bottle and work with hexane in a fume hood or designated work area well away from the Bunsen burner used in step 12. Avoid contact of all chemicals with eyes and skin. Wear chemical splash goggles and chemical-resistant gloves and apron. Wash hands thoroughly with soap and water before leaving the lab.

Stearic acid is a component of lipids (waxes, fats, and oils). It is used commercially as a waxy coating for pills and capsules.

Procedure

1. Prepare a boiling water bath for use in step 11: Half-fill a 150-mL beaker with water, add a boiling stone, and heat the beaker on a hot plate at a medium setting.

2. Label five weighing dishes and obtain 0.2–0.3 g samples of each solid in the appropriate weighing dish. Record the color and appearance of each solid in the data table.

3. Test the volatility and odor of each solid by wafting any vapors to your nose with your hand. Record all observations in the data table.

4. Test the conductivity of each solid by touching the wires of the conductivity tester directly to the solid. Record the conductivity of each sample in the data table.

5. Obtain a 24-well reaction plate and add a *small* amount of each solid (about the size of a grain of rice) to separate wells A1–A5, in the order shown in the data table.

6. Add about 20 drops of water to each well. Stir each mixture and observe whether the solid dissolves in water. Record the solubility (soluble, partially soluble, or insoluble) in the data table.

7. *For water-soluble substances only:* Determine the conductivity of the aqueous solution by placing the wires directly into the liquid. Record the results in the data table.

8. Label five small test tubes or a ceramic spot plate and add a small amount of each solid, about the size of a grain of rice, to separate test tubes.

9. Add about 20 drops of hexane to each test tube. Stir each mixture and observe whether the solid dissolves in hexane. Record the results in the data table.

10. Obtain a large, disposable aluminum evaporating dish or Pyrex® watch glass and place a small, pea-sized amount of each solid in separate locations on the dish.

11. Set the dish on top of the boiling water bath and heat the solids for 1–2 minutes. Observe whether any of the solids melt and record the observations in the data table.

12. *For solids that did not melt at the boiling water bath temperature:* Place a small, pea-sized amount of each solid in a clean and dry, Pyrex® test tube. Using a test tube holder, heat the test tube in a burner flame for 1–2 minutes. Record observations in the data table.

13. Test the brittleness of each solid by placing a small sample in the mortar designated for it and grinding with the pestle. Record the observations in the data table.

14. *(Optional)* Test the hardness of the mineral samples by trying to scratch them with a fingernail, a penny, and a nail. Record observations on the data sheet.

Teacher Notes

If several lab sections will be performing this experiment the same day, keep the boiling water baths (step 1) set up throughout the day. Use distilled or deionized water for best results and replenish the boiling stones as needed. Toothpicks are great micro-stirring rods for use in step 6. Do NOT place the aluminum evaporating dish used in step 10 in the Bunsen burner flame (step 12). Aluminum melts at 660 °C.

Teacher Notes

Name: _____

Class/Lab Period: _____

Properties of Solids

Data Table

Physical Property	Aluminum	Silicon Dioxide	Sodium Chloride	Stearic Acid	Sucrose
Color and Appearance					
Volatility and Odor					
Conductivity (Solid)					
Solubility in Water					
Conductivity of Aqueous Solution					
Solubility in Hexane					
Brittleness					
Melting Point*					

*The average temperature of a Bunsen burner flame is greater than 1000 °C.

(Optional) Use this space to write down your observations of the hardness of mineral samples.

Properties of Solids

Properties of Solids – Page 6

Post-Lab Questions *(Use a separate sheet of paper to answer the following questions.)*

1. Compare the volatility and odor of stearic acid and sucrose. Which is more volatile? Why? Is it possible for a compound to be volatile but have no odor? Explain.

2. Both stearic acid and sucrose are molecular substances, but one is polar and the other is nonpolar. Compare the solubility of the two compounds in water and in hexane to determine which is which.

3. Based on the answers to Questions #1 and 2, predict whether the intermolecular forces (forces between molecules) are stronger in polar or nonpolar substances.

4. In order for a substance to conduct electricity, it must have free-moving charged particles.

    (a) Explain the conductivity results observed for sodium chloride in the solid state and in aqueous solution.

    (b) Would you expect molten sodium chloride to conduct electricity? Why or why not?

    (c) Use the model of metallic bonding described in the *Background* section to explain why metals conduct electricity.

5. Name the three hardest substances that were tested. To what classes of solids do these substances belong? What general feature do these three types of solids have in common?

6. Compare the hardness and brittleness of aluminum versus salt. Suggest a reason, based on the crystal structure of metals versus ionic compounds, why hardness and brittleness are not the same thing.

7. Complete the following table (some of the entries have been filled in for you):

General Properties	Type of Solid			
	Covalent-network	Ionic	Metallic	Molecular
Melting Point			Low to high	
Solubility				Depends on polarity
Conductivity of Solid		Nonconductors		
Hardness	Very hard			
Brittleness				

Flinn ChemTopic™ Labs — Chemical Bonding

Teacher Notes

Teacher's Notes
Properties of Solids

Master Materials List *(for a class of 30 students working in pairs)*

Aluminum shot or granules, Al, 10 g
Distilled water and wash bottles, 15
Hexane, C_6H_{14}, 100 mL
Silicon dioxide (sand), SiO_2, 3–5 g
Sodium chloride (salt), NaCl, 3–5 g
Stearic acid, $C_{18}H_{36}O_2$, 3–5 g
Sucrose (sugar), $C_{12}H_{22}O_{11}$, 3–5 g
Minerals for hardness testing (optional)
   Aluminum foil or strip
   Candle (paraffin wax)
   Halite (sodium chloride)
   Quartz (silicon dioxide)
   Rock candy (sucrose)
Pennies and nails to test hardness (optional)
Balances, centigram, 3
Weighing dishes, 75

Aluminum evaporating dishes, 15
Beakers, 150-mL, 3–5*
Boiling stones
Bunsen burners, 3–5*
Conductivity testers, low-voltage, 3–5*
Hot plates, 3–5*
Mortars and pestles, ceramic, 5*
Pipets, Beral-type, 30
Reaction plates, 24-well, 15
Spatulas, 15
Stirring rods or toothpicks, 15
Test tubes, 13 × 100 mm, 75, or
   Ceramic spot plates, 15
Test tube racks, 15
Test tube holders (clamps), 15

*Students may share conductivity testers, hot plates (boiling water baths), laboratory burners, and mortars and pestles. Set up five mortars in a designated location and label them with the names of the solids to be tested.

Safety Precautions

Hexane is a flammable organic solvent and a dangerous fire risk. Keep away from flames, heat, and other sources of ignition. Cap the solvent bottle and work with hexane in a fume hood or designated work area well away from any Bunsen burners used in the lab. Avoid contact of all chemicals with eyes and skin. Wear chemical splash goggles and chemical-resistant gloves and apron. Please consult current Material Safety Data Sheets for additional safety, handling, and disposal information. Remind students to wash their hands thoroughly with soap and water before leaving the lab.

Disposal

Consult your current *Flinn Scientific Catalog/Reference Manual* for general guidelines and specific procedures governing the disposal of laboratory waste. The hexane solutions should be collected in a flammable organic waste container and allowed to evaporate according to Flinn Suggested Disposal Method #18a. All other solids and solutions may be disposed of in the trash according to Flinn Suggested Disposal Methods #26a and b, respectively.

Lab Hints

- The laboratory work for this experiment can easily be completed in a typical 50-minute lab period. The *Pre-Lab Questions* may be assigned as homework in preparation for lab or may be used as part of a class discussion prior to doing the lab.

Large solid or mineral samples needed for hardness testing are readily available for four out of the five solids used in this experiment. Consider using a candle or paraffin wax as a substitute for stearic acid in the optional hardness test. Both compounds are examples of nonpolar molecular solids. The recommended organic solvent is "hexanes"—a mixture of n-hexane and other C_6H_{14} isomers. Remind students not to use flammable organic solvents around or near a heat source.

Properties of Solids

Teacher's Notes

- Common solids with a wide range of physical properties were deliberately chosen for this study. There is enough overlap to be able to identify patterns in the relationship between the properties of a material and its structure. The challenge in this experiment comes as students try to use their observations to "see inside" the world of atoms and bonds. Using common household materials removes one (unnecessary) stumbling block in this process.

- Many other common solids may also be used. Any metal may be used instead of aluminum and many different ionic compounds may be substituted for sodium chloride. Suitable nonpolar organic solids that may be used instead of or in addition to stearic acid include lauric acid or paraffin wax.

- Low-voltage conductivity meters are available from Flinn Scientific (Catalog No. AP1493) for individual student use. The copper wire electrodes are about 2 cm long and are easily inserted into the wells on a microscale reaction plate. Two LEDs make it possible to compare the conductivity of strong versus weak electrolytes. The green LED requires more voltage than the red LED. A weak electrolyte will cause only the red LED to glow. A strong electrolyte will cause both the red and green LEDs to glow. Because the meter uses only a 9-volt battery, the conductivity tester is convenient, portable, and safe. Conductivity tests may also be done using conductivity sensors with a LabPro or CBL-2 computer interface system.

- Using a conventional 110-V "lightbulb-type" conductivity tester will require larger sample sizes. It is recommended that the teacher perform the conductivity tests as a demonstration if 110-V conductivity testers will be used.

- See the *Supplementary Information* section for a description of the Mohs hardness scale. (The information may be used as an optional student handout, if desired.) The Mohs hardness scale is a nonlinear, semiquantitative tool that is used in geology to rate the relative hardness of rocks and minerals. The scale ranges from 1 (talc) to 10 (diamond)—the higher the number, the harder the material. An object will only scratch something with a lower hardness rating.

- The following demonstration provides a good discrepant event to describe the hardness test. Ask students to predict what will happen if a nail is scraped across the glass stage on the overhead projector. After students have given their dire predictions, rub a nail back and forth on the overhead. The nail will not scratch the glass—steel (iron) has a hardness of 5 while glass has a hardness of 6. Always test this demonstration in one corner of the overhead projector first, however.

- Individual mineral samples (halite and quartz) suitable for hardness testing are available from Flinn Scientific. Consult with colleagues in the Science Department for mineral samples used in earth science or environmental science classes.

Teaching Tip

- See the experiment "It's in Their Nature" in *Solubility and Solutions,* Volume 12 in the Flinn ChemTopic™ Labs series, for a detailed investigation into the solubility of ionic, polar, and nonpolar compounds in a variety of solvents. Students classify compounds and learn about the different types of attractive forces that exist between molecules.

Teacher's Notes

Teacher Notes

Answers to Pre-Lab Questions *(Student answers will vary.)*

1. A student wanted to illustrate the structure of magnesium chloride and decided simply to replace the Na⁺ ions in Figure 1 with Mg^{2+} ions. What would be wrong with the resulting picture?

    The picture would show the wrong ratio of ions in the crystal structure. The formula of magnesium chloride is $MgCl_2$—there are two chloride ions for every magnesium ion. The ratio of positive and negative ions in the sodium chloride crystal structure is 1:1.

2. Covalent bonds may be classified as polar or nonpolar based on the difference in electronegativity between two atoms. Look up electronegativity values in your textbook:

    (a) Why are C—H bonds considered nonpolar?

    (a) The electronegativity values of carbon and hydrogen are similar (2.1 and 2.5, respectively.) Both atoms in a C—H bond have similar attractions for the bonding electrons and the bond is nonpolar.

    (b) Which is more polar, an O—H or N—H bond?

    (b) The electronegativity difference between O and H is greater (3.5 – 2.1) than that between N and H (3.0 – 2.1). An O—H bond is more polar than an N—H bond.

3. The three dimensional structure of diamond, a crystalline form of the element carbon, is shown in Figure 3. Use this structure to explain why diamond is the hardest known material.

    Diamond is a covalent-network solid. The structure consists of strong covalent carbon-carbon single bonds in all directions. Each carbon atom forms four bonds and thus has a stable octet of valence electrons. Cutting a diamond would require breaking many carbon–carbon bonds.

Figure 3.

Teacher's Notes

Sample Data

Teacher Notes

Student data will vary.

Data Table

Physical Property	Aluminum	Silicon Dioxide	Sodium Chloride	Stearic Acid	Sucrose
Color and Appearance	Shiny silver solid	Small, off-white crystals	White crystals	White flakes	Small white crystals
Volatility and Odor	Nonvolatile (no odor)	Nonvolatile (no odor)	Nonvolatile (no odor)	Volatile (waxy odor)	Nonvolatile (no odor)
Conductivity (Solid)	Strong conductor	Does not conduct electricity	Does not conduct electricity	Does not conduct electricity	Does not conduct electricity
Solubility in Water	Insoluble	Insoluble	Soluble	Insoluble	Soluble
Conductivity of Aqueous Solution	NA	NA	Strong conductor	NA	Does not conduct electricity
Solubility in Hexane	Insoluble	Insoluble	Insoluble	Soluble	Insoluble
Brittleness	Nonbrittle	Nonbrittle	Brittle	Brittle	Brittle
Melting Point*	Melts below 1000 °C†	Greater than 1000 °C	Melts ≈ 1000 °C†	Melts below 100 °C†	Melts >100 °C and burns

*The average temperature of a Bunsen burner flame is greater than 1000 °C. Microburners may not have as high a flame temperature.

†The melting point of sodium chloride (801 °C) is greater than that of pure aluminum metal (660 °C). Sodium chloride is observed to melt in a test tube placed in a Bunsen burner flame, while aluminum granules generally do not melt under these conditions. This is probably due to the invisible oxide coating which is always present on aluminum. The melting point of aluminum oxide is about 2000 °C.

Teacher's Notes

Teacher Notes

(Optional) Use this space to write down your observations of the hardness of mineral samples.

A candle can be scratched with a fingernail (Mohs hardness = 2).

Rock candy (sucrose) may also be scratched with a fingernail (Mohs hardness = 2).

Aluminum metal and a salt crystal can be scratched with a penny but not with a fingernail (Mohs hardness = 4).

A quartz (silicon dioxide) crystal can be scratched with a ceramic pestle but not with an iron nail (Mohs hardness = 7).

Answers to Post-Lab Questions *(Student answers will vary.)*

1. Compare the volatility and odor of stearic acid and sucrose. Which is more volatile? Why? Is it possible for a compound to be volatile but have no odor? Explain.

   Stearic acid has an odor and seems to be more volatile than sucrose. In order for a substance to have an odor, some molecules must enter the gas phase and diffuse in air to reach the nose. Some volatile substances, however, may not have an odor, because the nose lacks the appropriate receptors to "detect" the odor.

2. Both stearic acid and sucrose are molecular substances, but one is polar and the other is nonpolar. Compare the solubility of the two compounds in water and in hexane to determine which is which.

   Stearic acid dissolved in hexane, not in water. Sucrose dissolved in water, not in hexane. This suggests that stearic acid is nonpolar (like hexane), while sucrose is polar (like water). **Note to teachers:** *Stearic acid consists of a very long ($C_{17}H_{34}$—), nonpolar hydrocarbon "tail" attached to a small polar carboxylic acid (—CO_2H) group. The nonpolar hydrocarbon tail dominates the physical properties of the solid (solubility, melting point, etc.).*

3. Based on the answers to Questions #1 and 2, predict whether the intermolecular forces (forces between molecules) are stronger in polar or nonpolar substances.

   Polar substances have stronger intermolecular forces—it takes more energy to pull polar molecules apart and have molecules enter the gas phase.

4. In order for a substance to conduct electricity, it must have free-moving charged particles.

   (a) Explain the conductivity results observed for sodium chloride in the solid state and in aqueous solution.

   (a) Sodium chloride does not conduct electricity in the solid state. It has charged particles (ions) but the ions are "locked" into position in the crystal structure and are not able to move freely. A solution of sodium chloride in water does conduct electricity because the ions are no longer fixed into position. (The solute particles in a liquid are able to move freely.)

Properties of Solids

(b) Would you expect molten sodium chloride to conduct electricity? Why or why not?

(b) Molten sodium chloride should conduct electricity because the particles in a liquid are able to move freely.

(c) Use the model of metallic bonding described in the *Background* section to explain why metals conduct electricity.

(c) Metals conduct electricitiy because the valence electrons of the metal are not "attached" to any one metal atom. The electrons are delocalized among all of the metal cations in the crystal structure and are able to move freely throughout the crystal.

5. Name the three hardest substances that were tested. To what classes of solids do these substances belong? What general feature do these three types of solids have in common?

    The three hardest substances were aluminum (a metal), silicon dioxide (a covalent-network solid), and sodium chloride (an ionic compound). All of these solids have extended (infinite), three-dimensional crystal structures with strong bonds in all directions. There are no individual molecules in the solid state.

6. Compare the hardness and brittleness of aluminum versus salt. Suggest a reason, based on the crystal structure of metals versus ionic compounds, why hardness and brittleness are not the same thing.

    Aluminum is hard and nonbrittle. Salt is hard and brittle. The hardness of both solids is probably due to their extended, three-dimensional crystal structures. There are strong bonds in all directions and it is hard to apply enough force to break the bonds and dislocate an atom (or ion). Brittleness relates to what happens when particles in the solid state have been dislocated. The oppositely charged ions in the ionic lattice must occupy specific positions for optimum ionic bond strength. If some ions are displaced by force, attractive forces may be replaced by repulsive forces between ions of like charge. As a result, an ionic solid breaks or crumbles easily. In a metal, however, it does not matter if metal atoms are displaced by force, because all of the atoms are identical and the electrons can move around to minimize repulsion of the metal cations.

Teacher's Notes

Teacher Notes

7. Complete the following table:

General Properties	Type of Solid			
	Covalent-network	Ionic	Metallic	Molecular
Melting Point	Very high	High	Low to high	Low
Solubility	Insoluble in most solvents	Soluble in water	Insoluble in most solvents	Depends on polarity
Conductivity of Solid	Nonconductors	Nonconductors	Good conductors	Nonconductors
Hardness	Very hard	Hard	Soft to hard	Soft
Brittleness	Nonbrittle	Brittle	Nonbrittle	Brittle

Note to teachers: *Stress to students that these are general properties—there are many exceptions. The melting points of metals, for example, range from –39 °C (for mercury) to 3407 °C (for tungsten). Many low-melting metals (lithium, sodium, potassium, gallium, etc.) are also soft enough that they can be cut with a knife. Finally, not all ionic compounds are water-soluble.*

Teacher's Notes

Supplementary Information

Mohs Hardness Scale

Hardness is not an intrinsic or fundamental physical property of a substance. It is a defined property which can only be assessed by comparing the relative properties of two or more substances. Hardness is useful in mineralogy for the field identification of rocks and minerals.

Hardness is defined as the resistance of a mineral to being scratched. (This is different than breaking or shattering a mineral.) The geologist Friedrich Mohs developed a convenient scale for ranking minerals with respect to hardness. The principle behind the scale is quite simple—an object will only scratch something with a lower hardness rating. The scale and some common comparison tools are listed in the Table 1. Despite the obvious simplicity of the method, the scale actually gives pretty specific results. Thus, a penny will scratch a halite (salt) crystal, while a fingernail will not.

Hardness testing is extremely important in materials science and engineering for steel and other alloys, ceramics, and even plastics. Modern methods such as the Rockwell hardness test measure the depth or area of an indentation left by a diamond cone or a steel ball when a measured force is applied for a specified period of time.

Table 1. Mohs Hardness Scale

Hardness	Mineral	Comparison Tool
1	Talc	
2	Gypsum	Fingernail
3	Calcite	Copper penny
4	Fluorite	
5	Apatite	Iron nail
6	Feldspar	Glass
7	Quartz	Ceramic
8	Topaz	
9	Corundum	
10	Diamond	

*Page 1 – **Formula of an Ionic Compound***

Teacher Notes

Formula of an Ionic Compound
Balancing Charges on Ions

Introduction

Atoms of different elements combine with one another to form compounds. The empirical formula of an ionic compound indicates the kinds of atoms that are present in the compound as well as the relative number (ratio) of each kind of atom. Let's investigate how the formula of an ionic compound can be determined experimentally.

Concepts

- Ionic compounds
- Polyatomic ions
- Empirical formula
- Precipitation reaction

Background

An *ionic compound* is composed of ions—atoms or groups of atoms that have a positive or negative charge. Oppositely charged ions arrange themselves into an extended, three-dimensional structure called a crystal lattice. The net attractive forces among oppositely charged ions in the crystal structure are called ionic bonds. Although composed of charged ions, ionic compounds are electrically neutral. The ratio of oppositely charged ions in the crystal structure is such that the positive charge contributed by the cations is equal to or balanced by the negative charge contributed by the anions. There is no net or overall charge in an ionic compound.

The *empirical formula* of an ionic compound indicates the smallest whole number ratio of each type of ion in the crystal structure and is called a formula unit. For example, magnesium chloride has the empirical formula $MgCl_2$. Magnesium cations (Mg^{2+}) and chloride anions (Cl^-) combine in a 1:2 ratio to form the $MgCl_2$ formula unit. The overall charge on ionic compounds is always zero.

Some ions consist of a charged group of covalently bonded atoms. Such ions are called *polyatomic ions*. An example is the nitrate ion (NO_3^-), which contains one nitrogen atom and three oxygen atoms and has an overall charge of –1. In calcium nitrate, calcium (Ca^{2+}) ions combine with nitrate ions in a 1:2 ratio in order to balance the positive and negative charges. The empirical formula for calcium nitrate is $Ca(NO_3)_2$. Parentheses are used around the nitrate ion to show that the subscript "2" pertains to the nitrate ion as a whole.

Many ionic compounds can be prepared in the lab using *precipitation reactions*. When solutions of two ionic compounds are combined, the ions may rearrange to form a new ionic compound that is insoluble in water. An example of this type of reaction is the formation of solid barium sulfate when barium chloride and sodium sulfate are combined in solution (Equation 1a). In Equation 1b, only the ions that form the precipitate are represented. This makes it easier to recognize what happens in the precipitation reaction.

$$BaCl_2(aq) + Na_2SO_4(aq) \rightarrow BaSO_4(s) + 2NaCl(aq) \qquad \text{Equation 1a}$$

$$Ba^{2+}(aq) + SO_4^{2-}(aq) \rightarrow BaSO_4(s) \qquad \text{Equation 1b}$$

Precipitation reactions are an example of double replacement reactions. Depending on the placement of this activity in your curriculum, you may want to introduce or review the use of molecular equations, complete ionic equations, and net ionic equations to describe double replacement reactions.

Formula of an Ionic Compound – Page 2

According to the balanced equation for this reaction, barium ions (Ba^{2+}) combine with sulfate ions (SO_4^{2-}) in a 1:1 ratio to form barium sulfate ($BaSO_4$). This ratio can be observed experimentally in the lab by mixing $BaCl_2$(aq) and Na_2SO_4(aq) solutions containing equal amounts (concentrations) of barium and sulfate ions, respectively. The maximum amount of precipitate will be obtained when equal volumes (a 1:1 ratio) of the two solutions are combined. A similar approach can also be used to determine the formula of an unknown ionic compound.

Experiment Overview

The purpose of this experiment is to determine the empirical formula of an unknown ionic compound. Two solutions containing equal amounts (concentrations) of two reactant ions will be combined in a series of reactions. In each reaction, the total volume of the two solutions will be held constant while the volume ratio of the reactants is varied. The amount of precipitate obtained in each reaction will be measured and plotted against the volume ratio to find the empirical formula of the product.

Pre-Lab Questions

1. Many common drugstore chemicals are ionic compounds. Write the correct empirical formula for each of the following compounds.

Common name:	Milk of magnesia	Washing soda	Epsom salt
Chemical name:	Magnesium hydroxide	Sodium carbonate	Magnesium sulfate

2. Solutions of iron(III) chloride and sodium hydroxide were mixed in a series of precipitation reactions, as described in this experiment.

   (a) Name the two possible products in this precipitation reaction and predict their empirical formulas.

   (b) Which product is likely to be insoluble in water and precipitate out as a red solid?

   (c) What volume ratio of reactants gave the most precipitate (see Table 1)? Explain.

Table 1.

Test tube	1	2	3	4	5	6	7
$FeCl_3$, 0.1 M, mL	5	10	12	15	17	20	24
NaOH, 0.1 M, mL	55	50	48	45	43	40	36
Volume of precipitate, mL	1	10	14	20	4	1	0

Materials

Copper(II) chloride solution, $CuCl_2$, 0.1 M, 6 mL

Sodium phosphate solution, Na_3PO_4, 0.1 M, 6 mL

Marking pen or wax pencil

Metric ruler, marked in millimeters

Pipets, Beral-type, 2

Stirring rod or wood splints

Test tubes, small, 7

Test tube rack or 24-well reaction plate

Teacher Notes

See the Lab Hints *and* Teaching Tips *sections for a discussion of the results observed in the reaction of $FeCl_3$ and NaOH (Pre-Lab Question #2). The amounts of reagents shown in Table 1 are convenient for running this reaction as a demonstration for students prior to lab. The reactions may be carried out in 100-mL graduated cylinders.*

Flinn ChemTopic™ Labs — Chemical Bonding

Page 3 – **Formula of an Ionic Compound**

Teacher Notes

Safety Precautions

Copper(II) chloride and sodium phosphate solutions are skin and eye irritants and are slightly toxic by ingestion. Avoid contact of all chemicals with eyes and skin. Wear chemical splash goggles and chemical-resistant gloves and apron. Wash hands thoroughly with soap and water before leaving the lab.

Procedure

1. Label seven small test tubes #1–7 with a marking pen and place them in a test tube rack or in a 24-well reaction plate.

2. Cut the stems of two Beral-type pipets at a 45° angle about 5 cm from the bulb, as shown here.

3. Fill one pipet with 0.1 M copper(II) chloride solution and record the color of the solution in the data table.

4. Carefully add the appropriate number of drops of copper(II) chloride solution to each test tube #1–7, as shown in Table 2. *Note:* Exact volumes are very important—hold the pipet vertically to obtain uniform size drops.

5. Fill the second pipet with 0.1 M sodium phosphate solution and record the color of the solution in the data table.

6. Carefully add the appropriate number of drops of sodium phosphate solution to each test tube, as shown in Table 2.

Table 2.

Test tube	1	2	3	4	5	6	7
$CuCl_2$, 0.1 M (drops)	3	6	12	15	18	24	27
Na_3PO_4, 0.1 M (drops)	27	24	18	15	12	6	3

7. Use a *clean* stirring rod or wood splint to stir each reaction mixture in test tubes #1–7. Let the tubes sit undisturbed for 10–15 minutes to allow the precipitates to settle.

8. During this time, determine the volume (drop) ratio of copper(II) chloride and sodium phosphate solutions in each test tube. Write this ratio in the data table. *Example:* In test tube #1, 3 drops of $CuCl_2$ and 27 drops of Na_3PO_4 correspond to a 1:9 ratio of $CuCl_2$:Na_3PO_4.

9. After the precipitates have settled, observe the appearance of the products *(both the solid and the solution)*. Record the observations in the data table in the space provided. Be as detailed as possible.

10. Use a metric ruler to measure the height of the precipitate in millimeters in each test tube. Read from the top of the solid material to the bottom center of the test tube. Record each height in mm in the data table.

11. Dispose of the contents of the test tubes as directed by your instructor.

For best results, use 12 × 75 mm test tubes. If larger test tubes will be used, increase the total number of drops of solution proportionally. The solids in test tubes 1–7 settle well after 15 minutes (step 9).

Name: _____

Class/Lab Period: _____

Formula of an Ionic Compound

Data Table

Color of CuCl$_2$ Solution		Color of Na$_3$PO$_4$ Solution	
Appearance of Products			

Precipitation Reactions							
Test Tube	1	2	3	4	5	6	7
Volume Ratio* (Drops CuCl$_2$: Drops Na$_3$PO$_4$)	1:9						
Height of Precipitate (mm)							

*Reduce the volume ratio to the simplest whole-number ratio.

Post-Lab Questions

1. (a) Name the two possible products in the precipitation reaction of copper(II) chloride with sodium phosphate. Use the charges on the ions to predict the empirical formulas of the products.

   (b) Based on common knowledge, which product is likely to be insoluble in water and to precipitate from solution?

Teacher Notes

2. Complete the following bar graph to show the height of precipitate in each test tube.

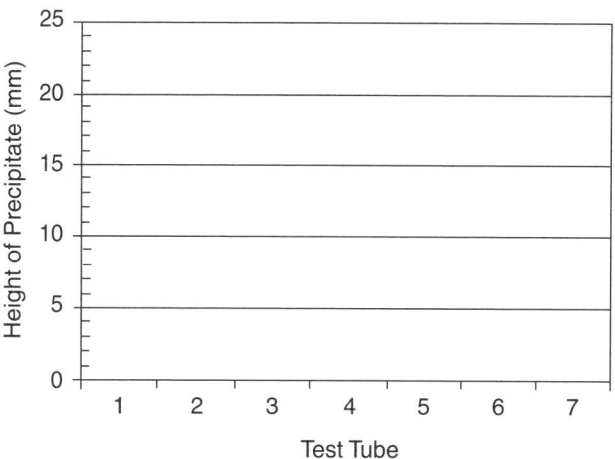

3. Which test tube had the greatest amount of precipitate? Does this result agree with the prediction made in Question #1 concerning the empirical formula of the product? Explain.

4. Write a balanced chemical equation for the precipitation reaction of copper(II) chloride and sodium phosphate. Include abbreviations for the physical state of each reactant and product, using (aq) for aqueous solution, (s) for solid, (l) for liquid, and (g) for gas.

5. (a) Which test tubes showed evidence of unreacted Cu^{2+} ions in the supernatant when the reaction was complete? Explain why unreacted Cu^{2+} ions were present in these tubes based on the volume ratio of solutions used.

Formula of an Ionic Compound – Page 6

5. (b) How could you tell that all of the Cu^{2+} ions had reacted in a particular test tube? Which test tubes showed such evidence? Explain, based on the volume ratio of solutions used.

6. What was the total number of drops of solution in each test tube? Why was it necessary to keep the total volume of reactants constant in each test tube?

7. *(Optional)* Does the *height* of precipitate in each test tube accurately reflect the *amount* of precipitate in each case? *Hint:* Compare the shape of a test tube to that of a graduated cylinder. What effect does this error have on the conclusions reached in this experiment?

Teacher Notes

Teacher Notes

Teacher's Notes
Formula of an Ionic Compound

Master Materials List *(for a class of 30 students working in pairs)*

Copper(II) chloride solution, $CuCl_2$, 0.1 M, 100 mL

Sodium phosphate solution, Na_3PO_4, 0.1 M, 100 mL

Marking pens or wax pencils, 15

Metric rulers, 15

Pipets, Beral-type, 30

Test tubes, 12 × 75 mm, 105*

Test tube racks or 24-well reaction plates, 15

Stirring rods, 15, or wood splints, 100

*For best results, use the smallest size test tubes available. If larger test tubes must be used, consider increasing the total number of drops of solutions used.

Preparation of Solutions *(for a class of 30 students working in pairs)*

Copper(II) Chloride, 0.1 M: Dissolve 1.7 g of copper(II) chloride dihydrate ($CuCl_2 \cdot 2H_2O$) in about 50 mL of distilled or deionized water. Stir to dissolve and then dilute to 100 mL with water.

Sodium Phosphate, 0.1 M: Dissolve 3.8 g of sodium phosphate dodecahydrate ($Na_3PO_4 \cdot 12H_2O$) in about 50 mL of distilled or deionized water. Stir to dissolve and dilute to 100 mL with water.

Safety Precautions

Copper(II) chloride and sodium phosphate solutions are skin and eye irritants and are slightly toxic by ingestion. Avoid contact of all chemicals with eyes and skin. Wear chemical splash goggles and chemical-resistant gloves and apron. Please consult current Material Safety Data Sheets for additional safety, handling, and disposal information. Remind students to wash their hands thoroughly with soap and water before leaving the lab.

Disposal

Consult your current *Flinn Scientific Catalog/Reference Manual* for general guidelines and specific procedures governing the disposal of laboratory waste. The waste solutions may be filtered to remove insoluble copper(II) phosphate, which may be disposed of in the trash according to Flinn Suggested Disposal Method #26a. The liquid waste may be washed down the drain with plenty of excess water according to Flinn Suggested Disposal Method #26b.

Lab Hints

- The laboratory work for this experiment can easily be completed in a typical 50-minute lab period. The lab works best if the solutions and precipitates are allowed to settle for at least 10–15 minutes. The *Pre-Lab Questions* may be assigned as homework in preparation for lab or may be used as part of a class discussion prior to doing the lab.

- Sample results for the reaction of iron(III) nitrate and sodium hydroxide were incorporated into the *Pre-Lab Questions* (see Table 1). This reaction may be carried out as a demonstration while the precipitates are settling. Notice that the amount of $Fe(OH)_3$ precipitate drops off quickly when excess iron(III) ions are used. As long as hydroxide

Copper(II) chloride is also called cupric chloride. Sodium phosphate may be called trisodium phosphate. Make sure you use Na_3PO_4 and not Na_2HPO_4 or NaH_2PO_4.

Teacher's Notes

ions are present in excess, the $Fe(OH)_3$ precipitate will settle out. When iron(III) ions are present in excess, however, the solution become acidic—the precipitate begins to dissolve and the solution turns dark red (as opposed to the initial yellow color of Fe(III) ions).

- This experiment has traditionally been carried out using lead iodide, which gives excellent results. Because of the toxicity of lead compounds, we do NOT recommend using PbI_2 in this experiment. Other precipitation reactions that are suitable for this activity include the reaction of copper(II) chloride with sodium hydroxide and the reaction of iron(III) nitrate with sodium phosphate. In the case of the reaction of copper(II) ions with hydroxide ions, the maximum amount of precipitate is correctly observed at a $Cu^{2+}:OH^-$ volume ratio of 1:2. The color of the solution is royal blue when excess hydroxide ions are present due to the formation of $Cu(OH)_n^{2-n}$ complex ions.

- Consider the following disposal procedure as an optional extension or follow-up to this activity. Prepare seven gravity filtration setups (labeled #1–7) with preweighed filter papers in a central location. At the conclusion of the experiment, have students pour their discarded reaction mixtures from test tubes #1–7 into the appropriately labeled funnels. When all of the products have been collected, rinse the solids and allow them to dry overnight. Weigh the amount of product collected in each funnel. Does the mass of precipitate obtained in each funnel corroborate the conclusions reached in this experiment? Which method is more accurate or valid?

Teaching Tips

- Depending on the placement of this activity in the curriculum, students will likely need help writing and balancing the chemical equation for the precipitation reaction. Also, this may be a good place to introduce or review the use of complete ionic and net ionic equations to describe double replacement reactions.

- See the demonstration "Stoichiometry and Solubility" in *Molar Relationships and Stoichiometry,* Volume 7 in the Flinn ChemTopic™ Labs series, for a large-scale, demonstration version of this activity. The demonstration utilizes two different precipitation reactions, both copper(II) chloride with sodium phosphate, as in this experiment, and iron(III) nitrate with sodium hydroxide (see the *Pre-Lab Questions*).

- An extended version of this activity featuring both of these reactions is also available as a student laboratory kit from Flinn Scientific (Chemical Formulas Kit, Catalog No. AP4569).

Teacher's Notes

Teacher Notes

Answers to Pre-Lab Questions *(Student answers will vary.)*

1. Many common drugstore chemicals are ionic compounds. Write the correct empirical formula for each of the following compounds.

Common name:	Milk of magnesia	Washing soda	Epsom salt
Chemical name:	Magnesium hydroxide	Sodium carbonate	Magnesium sulfate

   Magnesium hydroxide, $Mg(OH)_2$

   Sodium carbonate, Na_2CO_3

   Magnesium sulfate, $MgSO_4$

2. Solutions of iron(III) chloride and sodium hydroxide were mixed in a series of precipitation reactions, as described in this experiment.

   (a) Name the two possible products in this precipitation reaction and predict their empirical formulas.

   There are four ions present in solution when the reactants are combined: Fe^{3+}, Cl^-, Na^+, and OH^-. The two possible new ionic products formed via combination of these ions are iron(III) hydroxide [$Fe(OH)_3$], and sodium chloride (NaCl).

   (b) Which product is likely to be insoluble in water and precipitate out as a red solid?

   The precipitate is most likely iron(III) hydroxide, which is insoluble in water. The other product is sodium chloride (salt), which we know dissolves in water.

   (c) What volume ratio of reactants gave the most precipitate (see Table 1)? Explain.

   The greatest amount of precipitate (20 mL) was obtained when 15 mL of $FeCl_3$ was mixed with 45 mL of NaOH, that is, at a Fe^{3+}:OH^- volume ratio of 1:3. This supports our prediction that the empirical formula of the product is $Fe(OH)_3$.

Table 1.

Test tube	1	2	3	4	5	6	7
$FeCl_3$, 0.1 M, mL	5	10	12	15	17	20	24
NaOH, 0.1 M, mL	55	50	48	45	43	40	36
Volume of precipitate, mL	1	10	14	20	4	1	0

Teacher's Notes

Sample Data

Student data will vary.

Data Table

Color of CuCl$_2$ Solution	Blue-green	Color of Na$_3$PO$_4$ Solution	Clear and colorless
Appearance of Products	Mixing the solutions produced a heavy turquoise precipitate in all cases. The color of the remaining solution (supernatant) was different in different test tubes—in tubes #1–4, the supernatant was colorless. In tubes #5–7, the supernatant was light blue.		

Precipitation Reactions

Test Tube	1	2	3	4	5	6	7
Volume Ratio* (Drops CuCl$_2$:Drops Na$_3$PO$_4$)	1:9	1:4	2:3	1:1	3:2	4:1	9:1
Height of Precipitate (mm)	5	8	14	15	17	11	6

*Reduce the volume ratio to the simplest whole-number ratio.

Answers to Post-Lab Questions *(Student answers will vary.)*

1. (a) Name the two possible products in the precipitation reaction of copper(II) chloride with sodium phosphate. Use the charges on the ions to predict the empirical formulas of the products.

    There are four ions present in solution when the reactants are combined: Cu^{2+}, Cl^-, Na^+, and PO_4^{3-}. The two possible new ionic products formed via combination of these ions are copper(II) phosphate [$Cu_3(PO_4)_2$], and sodium chloride (NaCl).

   (b) Based on common knowledge, which product is likely to be insoluble in water and to precipitate from solution?

    The precipitate is most likely copper(II) phosphate. The other possible product is sodium chloride (salt), which is soluble in water.

Teacher's Notes

Teacher Notes

2. Complete the following bar graph to show the height of precipitate in each test tube.

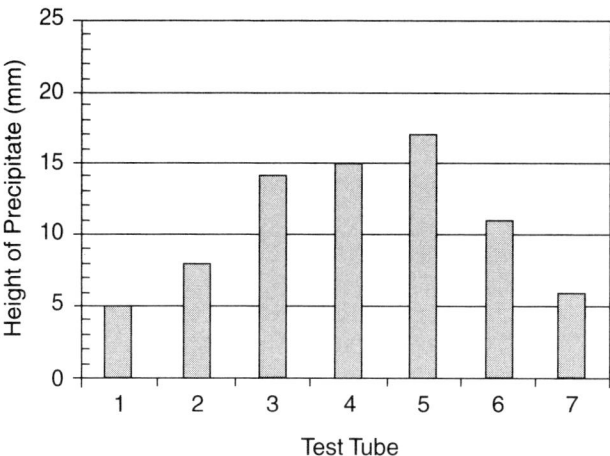

3. Which test tube had the greatest amount of precipitate? Does this result agree with the prediction made in Question #1 concerning the empirical formula of the product? Explain.

   The maximum amount of precipitate was observed in test tube #5, corresponding to a $CuCl_2:Na_3PO_4$ volume ratio of 3:2. This agrees with the prediction made in Question #1, namely, that the empirical formula of the product should be $Cu_3(PO_4)_2$. Three Cu^{2+} ions are needed to balance the charge of two PO_4^{3-} ions.

4. Write a balanced chemical equation for the precipitation reaction of copper(II) chloride and sodium phosphate. Include abbreviations for the physical state of each reactant and product, using (aq) for aqueous solution, (s) for solid, (l) for liquid, and (g) for gas.

   $3CuCl_2(aq) + 2Na_3PO_4(aq) \rightarrow Cu_3(PO_4)_2(s) + 6NaCl(aq)$

5. (a) Which test tubes showed evidence of unreacted Cu^{2+} ions in the supernatant when the reaction was complete? Explain why unreacted Cu^{2+} ions were present in these tubes based on the volume ratio of solutions used.

   In test tubes #6 and 7, the amount of sodium phosphate was less than that needed to combine with all of the copper(II) chloride (based on the required ion ratio in the product). "Leftover" copper(II) ions remained in solution after the precipitation reaction was complete in these test tubes and the final solutions were pale blue.

   (b) How could you tell that all of the Cu^{2+} ions had reacted in a particular test tube? Which test tubes showed such evidence? Explain, based on the volume ratio of solutions used.

   In test tubes #1–5, the amount of sodium phosphate solution was equal to or greater than the amount needed to react with all of the copper(II) chloride. The copper(II) ions were completely consumed in the precipitation reaction in these test tubes, and the final solutions were colorless.

Teacher's Notes

6. What was the total number of drops of solution in each test tube? Why was it necessary to keep the total volume of reactants constant in each test tube?

   A total of 30 drops of solution was added to each test tube. The total volume of solution was kept constant across the reaction series in order for the amount of precipitate to accurately reflect the number ratio of ions in solution. Imagine that two precipitation reactions are carried out, one starting with 10 mL of each solution, the other with 20 mL of each solution. The total amount of precipitate will obviously be greater in the second case—the maximum amount of product depends not only on the ratio of reactants but also on the total amount of each reactant.

7. *(Optional)* Does the *height* of precipitate in each test tube accurately reflect the *amount* of precipitate in each case? *Hint:* Compare the shape of a test tube to that of a graduated cylinder. What effect does this error have on the conclusions reached in this experiment?

   The height of precipitate does not accurately reflect the amount of precipitate formed in each test tube. Because the bottom of a test tube is curved, a test tube containing 10 mm of a precipitate will have more than twice the amount of precipitate as a test tube containing 5 mm of precipitate. This error is not significant for this experiment because we were only looking for the maximum amount of precipitate and the error was the same in all the test tubes across the series.

Teacher Notes

Lewis Structures and Molecular Geometry
Models of Covalent Bonding

Introduction
Molecules have shape! The structure and shape of a molecule influences its physical properties and affects its chemical behavior as well. Lewis structures and VSEPR theory offer useful models for visualizing the structures of covalent compounds.

Concepts
- Valence electrons
- Lewis structures
- Covalent bonding
- VSEPR theory

Background
Covalent bonds are defined as the net attractive forces between nonmetal atoms that share one, two, or three pairs of electrons. In general, only the *valence electrons,* those in the highest energy levels that are farthest away from the nucleus, are available for bonding. The number of valence electrons influences the number of bonds that an atom will form. The periodic table offers a convenient shortcut for determining the number of valence electrons in an atom. Remember that the position of an element in the modern periodic table reflects its electron configuration. When the representative elements are arranged in columns from IA to VIIIA (Figure 1), the number of valence electrons for an element is equal to its group number. Thus, potassium in Group IA has one valence electron, carbon in Group IVA has four valence electrons, and chlorine in Group VIIA has seven valence electrons. In 1916, G. N. Lewis, an American chemist, proposed arranging dots around the symbols of the elements to represent the valence electrons. *Lewis electron-dot symbols* (Figure 2) remain the most popular way to picture the valence electrons that are available for bonding.

According to the most recent, official IUPAC recommendations, the columns in the periodic table are numbered continuously from 1–18, with no breaks for the transition metals. The A/B Roman numeral numbering system (Figure 1) is often still shown in textbooks, probably because it helps students predict valence electrons and ionic charges.

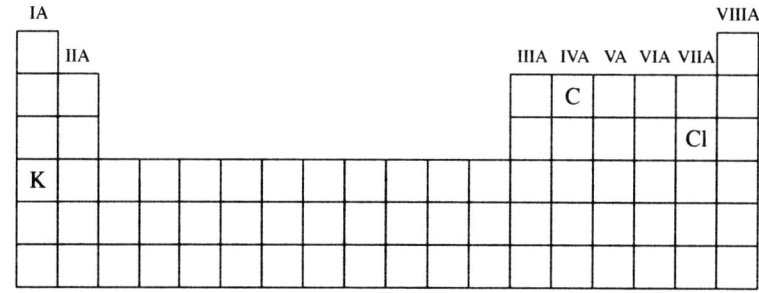

Figure 1. Numbering of Representative Elements in Groups IA–VIIIA.

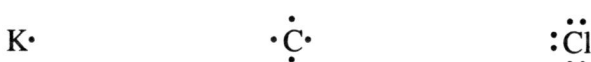

Figure 2. Lewis Electron-Dot Symbols for Representative Elements.

Lewis structures build on the Lewis electron-dot symbols of the elements to show the bonding arrangement of atoms in a molecule and the distribution of all valence electrons. The Lewis structure of a molecule thus shows all of the atoms and how they are connected. A single covalent bond between two atoms, corresponding to a pair of electrons, is represented using a dash (—). Sometimes atoms share more than one pair of electrons between them in order to form stable molecules. Two dashes, corresponding to two pairs of electrons, and three dashes, corresponding to three pairs of electrons, are used to represent double and triple bonds, respectively.

G. N. Lewis offered a simple theory, based on the known stability of the noble gases (He, Ne, etc.), to predict how many bonds an atom will form and how many atoms of a particular type will come together to form a stable molecule. According to Lewis, nonmetals may share electrons in order to achieve a valence shell electron "count" similar to that of the noble gases:

> *"Two atoms may conform to the rule of eight, or the octet rule . . .*
> *by sharing one or more pairs of electrons. The electrons which*
> *are held in common by two atoms may be considered to belong*
> *to the outer shell of both atoms."*

The noble gases have filled s and p orbitals with eight electrons. The octet rule assumes that atoms form molecules to achieve this stable, noble gas electron configuration. In counting valence electrons in order to predict the structure of a covalent compound, we will distinguish between two kinds of electron pairs. *Bonding pairs* of electrons are shared between atoms and thus "belong" to both atoms in the bond. *Nonbonding* or *unshared pairs* of electrons are not shared between atoms and are therefore "counted" toward only one of the atoms. Consider the fluorine molecule (F_2). Each fluorine atom has seven valence electrons and needs only one more electron to form a stable molecule—two fluorine atoms come together and share one bonding pair of electrons (Equation 1). Each fluorine atom retains its three unshared pairs of electrons.

$$:\!\ddot{F}\!\cdot \;+\; \cdot\!\ddot{F}\!: \longrightarrow :\!\ddot{F}\!:\!\ddot{F}\!:$$

Equation 1

$$:\!\ddot{F}\!-\!\ddot{F}\!:$$

Lewis Structure of Fluorine

Molecular Geometry

According to the **V**alence **S**hell **E**lectron **P**air **R**epulsion (VSEPR) theory, the valence electron pairs that surround an atom repel each other due to their like negative charges. In order to minimize this repulsion, the electron pairs should be positioned around the atom so that they are as far apart as possible. The resulting symmetrical arrangement of electron pairs around atoms can be used to predict molecular geometry—the three-dimensional shape of a molecule. Two pairs of electrons around an atom should adopt a linear arrangement, three pairs a trigonal planar arrangement, and so on.

The three-dimensional structure of a molecule is affected by the spatial arrangement of *all* the electron pairs—both bonding and nonbonding—around the central atom. However, only the physical arrangement of the *atoms* is used to describe the resulting molecular geometry.

Teacher Notes

Students may refer to their textbooks for additional examples, drawings, and models of molecular geometry. We recommend, however, that students start with the actual physical models used in Part B to learn about VSEPR theory and molecular geometry. Words and pictures on the printed page are not an adequate substitute for students holding the models in their hands as they try to visualize the shapes of molecules.

Teacher Notes

Page 3 – Lewis Structures and Molecular Geometry

This is best illustrated using an example. The Lewis structure of the water molecule is shown in Figure 3—there are four pairs of valence electrons around the central oxygen atom. Two pairs of electrons are involved in bonding to hydrogen atoms, while the other two electron pairs are unshared pairs. Four pairs of electrons around an atom will adopt a tetrahedral arrangement in space, as depicted in Figure 3, to be as far apart in space as possible. As a result, the two hydrogen atoms and the oxygen atom occupy a "bent" (inverted-V) arrangement.

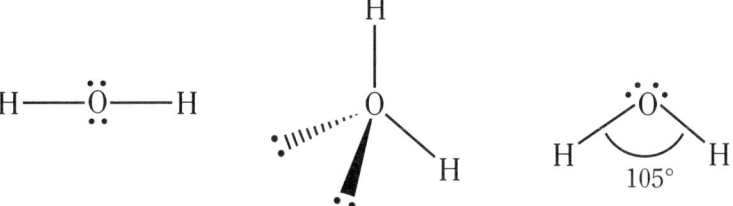

Figure 3. Lewis Structure of Water and Its Molecular Geometry.

When two atoms are linked via a double or triple bond (with two or three bonding pairs of electrons, respectively), the multiple electron pairs between the atoms must be considered together when determining the shape of the molecule. Carbon dioxide provides a good example (Figure 4). The central carbon atom is linked to two oxygen atoms by two double bonds. The resulting arrangement of atoms is linear—both electron pairs in each double bond are considered to be an electron group that must be in approximately the same region, near the oxygen atom.

Figure 4. Lewis Structure of Carbon Dioxide and Its Molecular Geometry.

Experiment Overview

The purpose of this activity is to practice drawing Lewis structures of molecules and to use these structures to predict their molecular geometry. Molecular models will be studied to visualize the shapes of molecules and to sketch their three-dimensional structures.

Pre-Lab Questions

1. Write the Lewis electron-dot symbol for each of the following atoms: hydrogen, boron, nitrogen, silicon, sulfur, and bromine.

2. What information about a molecule does its Lewis structure provide? What information is neither shown nor implied in the Lewis structure?

3. There are several exceptions to the octet rule.

    (a) Based on its electron configuration, explain why hydrogen can only have two valence electrons around it when it bonds to other atoms. What is the maximum number of bonds hydrogen will form?

Continued on next page

Lewis Structures and Molecular Geometry – Page 4

(b) Neutral compounds of boron may be described as "electron-deficient." Based on its electron configuration, predict how many covalent bonds boron will form. Is this the maximum number of bonds boron will form? *Hint:* Boron forms polyatomic ions.

(c) Many elements in the third row and beyond in the periodic table may form more than four bonds and thus appear to have "expanded octets." Phosphorus and sulfur, for example, may form five and six covalent bonds, respectively. Count up the total number of valence electrons in PCl_5 and draw its Lewis structure. How many valence electrons are "counted" toward the central P atom?

Materials

Periodic table
Set of molecular models labeled A through K

Safety Precautions

Although this activity is considered nonhazardous, observe all normal laboratory safety guidelines.

Procedure

Part A. Lewis Structures

1. Write the formula for each molecule or polyatomic ion listed in Data Table A. Some of the formulas have been filled in for you.

2. Count the number of valence electrons supplied by each atom in the formula. Determine the *total number* of valence electrons and record this number in Data Table A. In the case of polyatomic ions, *add* one electron for each unit of *negative* charge or *subtract* one electron for each unit of *positive* charge to determine the total number of valence electrons.

3. Use the following guidelines to draw a reasonable Lewis structure for each molecule or ion in the space provided. If more than one Lewis structure is reasonable, draw all of the appropriate Lewis structures. *Note:* Keep in mind the exceptions to the octet rule discussed in the *Pre-Lab Questions*.

- Draw a "skeleton" structure for the molecule or ion, joining atoms by single bonds. If there is a single atom of one element in a compound, show it as the *central atom* with other atoms joined to it. Hydrogen is never a central atom. The least electronegative atom is usually the central atom.

- From the total number of valence electrons, subtract two for each single bond in the skeleton—this tells you how many valence electrons are left to distribute.

Example:
$COCl_2$ has 24 valence electrons.

$$Cl-\underset{\underset{Cl}{|}}{\overset{\overset{O}{|}}{C}}$$

$24 - (3 \times 2) =$ 18 valence electrons must be distributed.

Teacher Notes

Teacher Notes

- Use the octet rule to distribute the remaining valence electrons as unshared pairs around the atoms in the molecule or ion.

- If this point is reached and there are too few valence electrons to give each atom an octet, multiple bond(s) may be needed. Remember that bonding electrons are "counted" toward both atoms in the bond, while unshared electrons are "assigned" to only one atom.

- If all else fails, some Lewis structures can only be drawn by assuming there is an unpaired electron in the molecule.

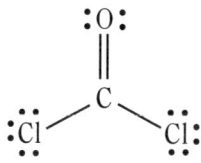

C atom does not have an octet.
C forms double bond to O atom.

N/A

Part B. Molecular Models

4. Examine the molecular models A–K. For each model, identify the number of bonding pairs, the number of unshared pairs, and the total number of electron pairs around the *central atom*. Record this information in Data Table B. *Note:* In the case of double or triple bonds, count all of the electrons involved in the bond as *one pair* of electrons. (Review the structure of carbon dioxide in the *Background* section.)

5. Sketch the three-dimensional arrangement of valence electron pairs around each central atom in Data Table B. Recall that multiple pairs of bonding electrons in double and triple bonds must "point" to the same atom.

6. Use the following terms to describe the *molecular geometry* for each model: Linear, trigonal planar, bent, tetrahedral, pyramidal, trigonal bipyramidal, octahedral, square pyramidal, and square planar. Record the molecular geometry in Data Table B. *Hint:* Molecular geometry describes the physical arrangement of the atoms, not the electron pairs.

Students may struggle with how the VSEPR model is used to predict the shapes of molecules containing multiple bonds (see step 4, Part B). Each multiple bond is treated as though it were a single electron pair. This is because all electron pairs of a multiple bond are required to be in approximately the same region of space.

7. *Return to the molecules and polyatomic ions listed in Data Table A.* Refer to the models from Part B for comparison: Count the number of valence electron pairs (see step 4) around the central atom and predict the molecular geometry for each molecule or ion in Data Table A.

8. Draw a three-dimensional sketch of the molecule or ion in the space below its name and describe its molecular geometry (see step 6) in Data Table A. *Example:* The structure of H_2O could be sketched as follows.

Name: _____

Class/Lab Period: _____

Lewis Structures and Molecular Geometry

Data Table A

Name	Molecular Formula	Valence Electrons	Lewis Structure
Boron Trichloride			
Methane			
Ethylene	C_2H_4		
Ammonia			
Ammonium Ion			
Hydrogen Sulfide			

Teacher Notes

Teacher Notes

Data Table A (continued)

Name	Molecular Formula	Valence Electrons	Lewis Structure
Sulfur Trioxide			
Acetylene	C_2H_2		
Phosphorus Trichloride			
Carbon Tetrachloride			
Iodine Pentafluoride			
Carbonate Ion			
Thiocyanate Ion	SCN^-		

Data Table A (continued)

Name	Molecular Formula	Valence Electrons	Lewis Structure
Carbon Disulfide			
Formaldehyde	H_2CO		
Sulfate Ion			
Arsenic Pentafluoride			
Hydrogen Cyanide			
Sulfur Hexafluoride			
Xenon Tetrafluoride			

Teacher Notes

Page 9 – **Lewis Structures and Molecular Geometry**

Data Table B

Model	Bonding Pairs*†	Unshared Pairs*	Total Pairs	Sketch and Molecular Geometry
A				
B				
C				
D				
E				
F				
G				
H				
I				
J				
K				

*Count the bonding and nonbonding pairs of electrons around the central atom only.
†In the case of double or triple bonds, count all of the electrons involved in the bond as one pair of electrons.

Teacher's Notes
Lewis Structures and Molecular Geometry

Master Materials List *(for a class of 30 students working in groups)*

Periodic Tables, 30

Sets of molecular models labeled A–K, 3*

*Having three sets of models available will make the lab more effective. Students need time to examine the models carefully, count electron pairs, and sketch three-dimensional structures.

Safety Precautions

Although this activity is considered nonhazardous, observe all normal laboratory safety guidelines.

Disposal

None required.

Lab Hints

- This is a paper-and-pencil activity—two class sessions are recommended for its completion. Students may work on Lewis structures (Part A) one day, examine and sketch models (Part B) in class another day, and then complete the sketches of the molecules needed for Part A out of class, if desired. Since this is a dry-lab exercise, students may work individually. Having students work collaboratively in groups of two or three, however, will provide a better learning environment, making it easier for students to brainstorm and run ideas back and forth.

- Many different kinds of model sets may be used to build the molecular models required for Part B. Inexpensive homemade models may also be constructed using different size Styrofoam balls and pipe cleaners or wires. See the *Supplementary Information* section for photos of the models required for this activity. If enough model sets are available, consider having students build their own models.

- The plastic models illustrated on pp. 41–42 were built using the "Shapes of Molecules Model Set" (Catalog No. AP5456) and the "Inorganic/Organic Teacher Model Set" (Catalog No. AP5455) available from Flinn Scientific. Replacement atoms and bonds for the "Inorganic/Organic Model Set" are also available. The "Shapes of Molecules" set may be used to prepare one model for each of the principal types of molecular geometries (linear, bent, trigonal planar, pyramidal, tetrahedral, trigonal bipyramidal, octahedral, square pyramidal and square planar). Notice that the "Shapes of Molecules Model Set" shows both bonding and nonbonding electron pairs but does not show double and triple bonds. With the "Inorganic/Organic Teacher Model Set," it is possible to represent double and triple bonds as distinct from single bonds, if this is desired.

- Data Tables A and B are provided in this book for the teacher's convenience. Because the tables use up a lot of paper, however, teachers may prefer to have students prepare their own tables. The sample tables may be used as templates—the teacher may wish to prepare overhead transparencies of Data Tables A and B.

Teacher Notes

Teaching Tips

- Many teachers have developed their own protocols for drawing Lewis structures. There are no hard-and-fast rules. One approach that works well is to study the typical number of bonds that an atom will form when it has zero formal charge—carbon forms four bonds, nitrogen three bonds, oxygen two bonds, fluorine one bond, etc. Drawing Lewis structures always requires trial-and-error, however, no matter how detailed the "rules" that the students are given.

- Having students sketch three-dimensional structures of molecules is an important part of this activity. The spatial reasoning skills required to visualize molecules in three dimensions will vary greatly across the student population. All students will benefit from the opportunity to hold models in their hands, rotate them, turn them upside down, etc. Some students, for example, will have no trouble at all "following the rules" and drawing Lewis structures for molecules. They may need more time, however, to see the molecules in three dimensions and to identify why different molecules share the same molecular geometry. Another group of students may proceed more slowly through the Lewis structures but will be able to recognize three-dimensional structures with ease.

Answers to Pre-Lab Questions *(Student answers will vary.)*

1. Write the Lewis electron-dot symbol for each of the following atoms: hydrogen, boron, nitrogen, silicon, sulfur, and bromine.

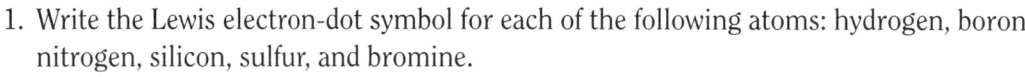

   Note to teachers: There are no rules for where the dots are drawn.

2. What information about a molecule does its Lewis structure provide? What information is neither shown nor implied in the Lewis structure?

   The Lewis structure shows all of the atoms in a molecule and how they are connected via single, double or triple bonds. It also shows any unshared pairs of valence electrons on each atom in the structure. The Lewis structure does not provide any information concerning the three-dimensional structure of the molecule or bond angles between atoms. The structures are drawn in two dimensions and are not meant to be perspective drawings.

3. There are several exceptions to the octet rule.

   (a) Based on its electron configuration, explain why hydrogen can only have two valence electrons around it when it bonds to other atoms. What is the maximum number of bonds hydrogen will form?

   Hydrogen has one valence electron in a 1s orbital. The 1s orbital can accommodate only two electrons and there are no p orbitals in the n = 1 principal energy level. Therefore, hydrogen can have only two electrons around it when it bonds to other atoms. Hydrogen can form a maximum of one (single) covalent bond.

Teacher's Notes

(b) Neutral compounds of boron may be described as "electron-deficient." Based on its electron configuration, predict how many covalent bonds boron will form. Is this the maximum number of bonds boron will form? *Hint:* Boron forms polyatomic ions.

The valence electron configuration of boron is $2s^22p^1$. Boron has three valence electrons available for bonding and thus should form only three covalent bonds by sharing these electrons with other atoms. In neutral compounds, if one "counts" bonding electrons as belonging to both atoms in the bond, then boron would have six electrons around it, not eight. Because the outermost $n = 2$ principal energy level for boron will accommodate a total of eight electrons, it is possible for boron to form four covalent bonds if it "accepts" additional electrons. The borohydride (BH_4^-) and fluoroborate (BF_4^-) anions are examples of polyatomic ions in which boron forms four bonds.

(c) Many elements in the third row and beyond in the periodic table may form more than four bonds and thus appear to have "expanded octets." Phosphorus and sulfur, for example, may form five and six covalent bonds, respectively. Count up the total number of valence electrons in PCl_5 and draw its Lewis structure. How many valence electrons are "counted" toward the central P atom?

PCl_5 has a total of 40 valence electrons distributed as shown in the following Lewis structure. The phosphorus atom forms five bonds to chlorine atoms and by the electron counting scheme appears to have 10 electrons in its valence shell. This is permitted because the P atom has empty 3d orbitals.

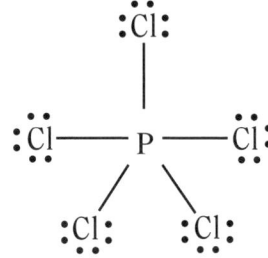

Teacher Notes

Sample Data

Data Table A

Name		Molecular Formula	Valence Electrons	Lewis Structure
Boron Trichloride	Trigonal Planar	BCl_3	24	$:\ddot{C}l - B - \ddot{C}l:$ with $:\ddot{C}l:$ below B
Methane	Tetrahedral	CH_4	8	H—C—H with H above and below
Ethylene	Trigonal Planar	C_2H_4	12	H—C=C—H with H's below
Ammonia	Pyramidal	NH_3	8	H—N̈—H with H below
Ammonium Ion	Tetrahedral	NH_4^+	8	[H—N—H with H above and below]$^+$
Hydrogen Sulfide	Bent	H_2S	8	H—S̈—H

Lewis Structures and Molecular Geometry

Teacher's Notes

Data Table A (continued)

Name	Molecular Formula	Valence Electrons	Lewis Structure
Sulfur Trioxide (Trigonal Planar)	SO_3	24	Three resonance structures: $:\ddot{O}=S(-\ddot{O}:)(-\ddot{O}:)$ ↔ ↔ (resonance of S=O double bond among three oxygens)
Acetylene (Linear)	C_2H_2	10	H—C≡C—H
Phosphorus Trichloride (Pyramidal)	PCl_3	26	$:\ddot{C}l—\ddot{P}—\ddot{C}l:$ with $:\ddot{C}l:$ below P
Carbon Tetrachloride (Tetrahedral)	CCl_4	32	C bonded to four $:\ddot{C}l:$ groups
Iodine Pentafluoride (Square Pyramidal)	IF_5	42	I bonded to five $:\ddot{F}:$ groups with lone pair
Carbonate Ion (Trigonal Planar)	CO_3^{2-}	24	Three resonance structures of $[CO_3]^{2-}$
Thiocyanate Ion (Linear)	SCN^-	16	$[:\ddot{S}—C≡N:\;\leftrightarrow\;:\ddot{S}=C=\ddot{N}:]^-$

Flinn ChemTopic™ Labs — Chemical Bonding

Teacher's Notes

Teacher Notes

Data Table A (continued)

Name		Molecular Formula	Valence Electrons	Lewis Structure
Carbon Disulfide Linear		CS_2	16	$\ddot{\underset{..}{S}}=C=\ddot{\underset{..}{S}}$
Formaldehyde Trigonal Planar		H_2CO	12	H—C(=Ö)—H
Sulfate Ion Tetrahedral		SO_4^{2-}	32	$[O-S(O)(O)-O \leftrightarrow O-S(O)(O)-O]^{2-}$
Arsenic Pentafluoride Trigonal Bipyramidal		AsF_5	40	F—As(F)(F)(F)—F
Hydrogen Cyanide Linear		HCN	10	H—C≡N:
Sulfur Hexafluoride Octahedral		SF_6	48	F—S(F)(F)(F)(F)—F
Xenon Tetrafluoride Square Planar		XeF_4	36	F—Xe(F)(F)—F

Only one of the double-bonded resonance forms is shown for the sulfate ion. The double-bonded forms are preferred from a formal charge viewpoint, but are not required to satisfy the octet rule. Notice that the sulfur atom has an expanded octet in these forms.

Lewis Structures and Molecular Geometry

Teacher's Notes

Data Table B

Teacher Notes

Model	Bonding Pairs*†	Unshared Pairs*	Total	Sketch and Molecular Geometry
A	2	0	2	Linear
B	2	0	2	Linear
C	3	0	3	Trigonal planar
D	3	0	3	Trigonal planar
E	4	0	4	Tetrahedral
F	3	1	4	Trigonal pyramidal
G	2	2	4	Bent
H	5	0	5	Trigonal bipyramidal
I	5	1	6	Square pyramidal
J	6	0	6	Octahedral
K	4	2	6	Square planar

*Count the bonding and nonbonding pairs of electrons around the central atom only.

†In the case of double or triple bonds, count all of the electrons involved in the bond as one pair of electrons.

Flinn ChemTopic™ Labs — Chemical Bonding

Teacher's Notes

Teacher Notes

Supplementary Information

Molecular Models Required for Part B

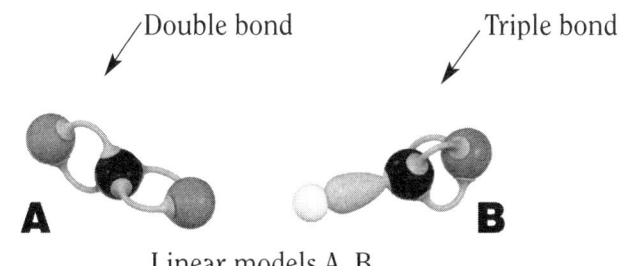

Linear models A, B

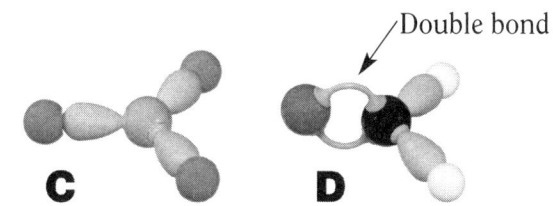

Trigonal planar models, C, D

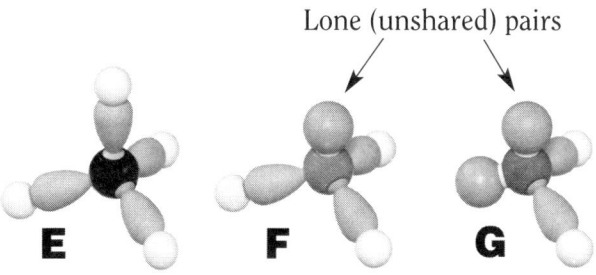

Tetrahedral, pyramidal, and bent models E, F, G

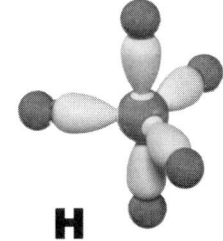

Trigonal bipyramidal model H

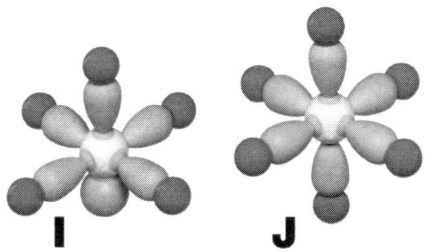

Square pyramidal, octahedral, and square planar models I, J, K

Teacher's Notes

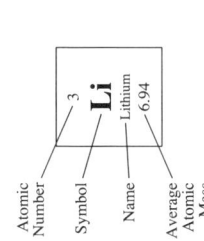

Periodic Table of the Elements

Flinn ChemTopic™ Labs — Chemical Bonding

Teacher Notes

The Color of Chemistry
Dyes, Dyeing, and Chemical Bonding

Introduction

The art of dyeing dates back thousands of years to the use of natural dyes extracted from plants and animals. Some dyes, such as Tyrian purple obtained from shellfish, were so rare that only emperors and kings could afford to wear purple—hence the term "royal purple." The modern dye industry started 150 years ago with the discovery of "mauve," the first synthetic dye. Since then, thousands of dyes have been developed to work with all types of fabrics.

Concepts

- Chemical bonding
- Ionic bonds
- Polar vs. nonpolar bonds
- Hydrogen bonding

Background

Dyes are organic compounds that can be used to impart bright, permanent colors to fabrics. The affinity of a dye for a fabric depends on the chemical structure of the dye and fabric molecules and on the interactions between them. Chemical bonding thus plays an important role in how and why dyes work.

The chemical structures of six common fabrics—wool, acrylic, polyester, nylon, cotton, and acetate—are shown in Figure 1. Cotton and wool are natural fibers obtained from plants and animals, while acrylic, polyester, and nylon are synthetic fibers made from petrochemicals. Acetate, also called cellulose acetate, is prepared by chemical modification of natural cellulose. All of the fabrics, whether natural or synthetic, are polymers. These are high molecular weight, long chain molecules made up of multiple repeating units of small molecules. The structures of the repeating units are enclosed in brackets in Figure 1. The number of repeating units *(n)* varies depending on the fiber and how it is prepared.

Wool is a protein, a naturally occurring polymer made up of amino acid repeating units. Many of the amino acid units have acidic or basic side chains that are ionized (charged). The presence of many charged groups in the structure of wool provides excellent binding sites for dye molecules, most of which are also charged. Cotton is a polysaccharide composed of glucose units attached to one other in a very rigid structure. The presence of three polar hydroxyl (–OH) groups per glucose repeating unit provides multiple sites for hydrogen bonding to ionic and polar groups in dye molecules. Acetate is cellulose in which some of the –OH groups have been replaced by acetate groups (–OCOCH$_3$). The presence of acetate side chains makes acetate softer and easier to work with than cotton but also provides fewer binding sites for dye molecules.

Nylon was the first completely synthetic polymer fiber. It is a polyamide, made up of hydrocarbon repeating units joined together by highly polar amide (–CONH–) functional groups. The amide groups provide sites for hydrogen bonding to dye molecules. The repeating units in polyester are joined together by ester (–COO–) functional groups. Finally, acrylic fiber is poly(acrylonitrile). Each repeating unit contains one nitrile (–C≡N) functional group.

This lab offers a perfect opportunity to present chemistry in its historical context and also to highlight the role of chemistry in consumer applications. Encourage students to research the fascinating early history of natural dyes and dyeing—there are some great stories. For a well-reviewed book about the impact of mauve on the history and development of science, see Mauve: How One Man Invented a Color that Changed the World, *by Simon Garfield.*

Teacher Notes

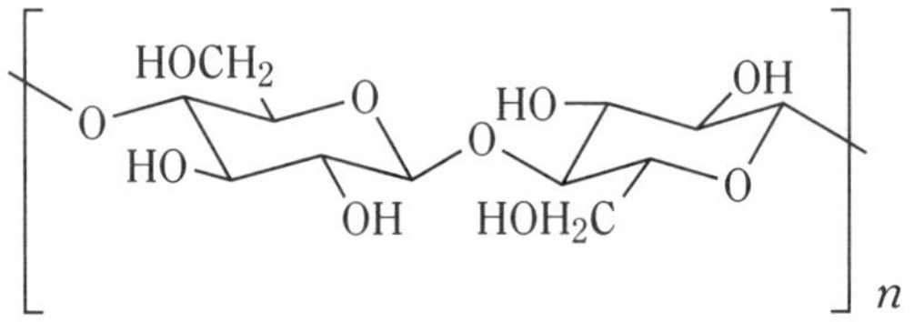

Cotton (Cellulose)

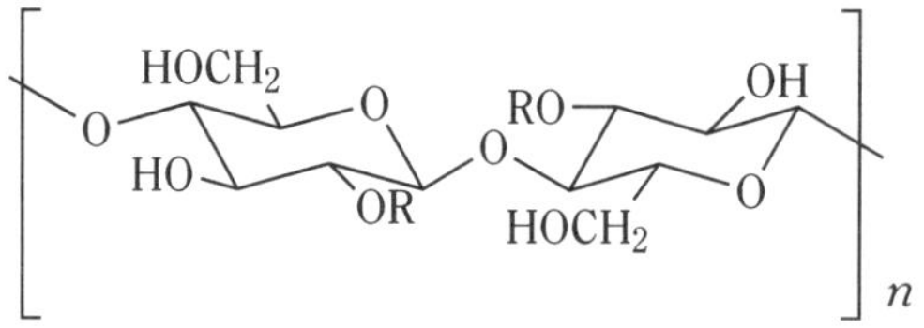

Cellulose Acetate (R = $COCH_3$)

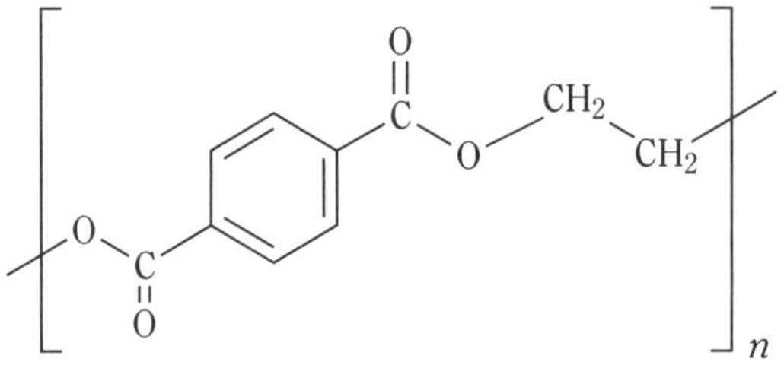

Polyester (Dacron)

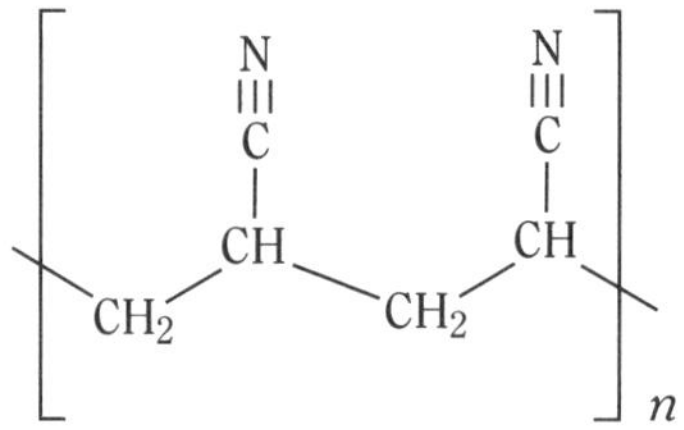

Acrylic (Orlon)

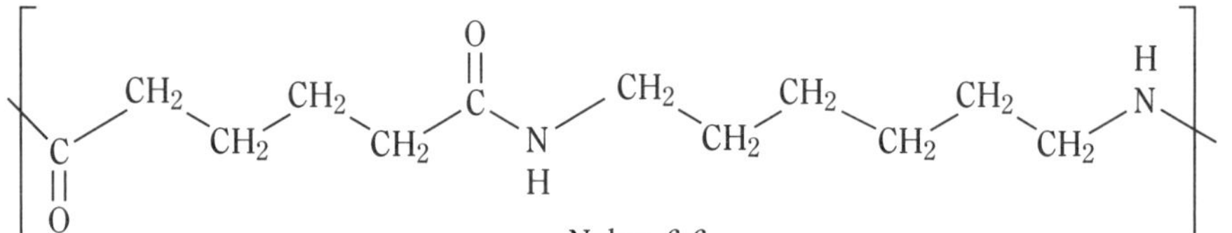

Nylon-6,6

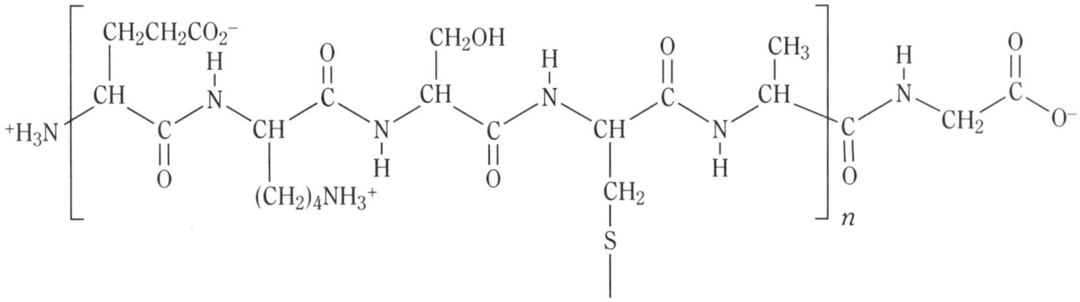

Wool (Protein)

Figure 1. Chemical Structures of Fabric Molecules.

Dyes are classified based on both the structure of the dye and the way in which the dye is applied to the fabric.

- *Direct dyes* are charged, water-soluble organic compounds that bind to ionic and polar sites on fabric molecules. Direct dye molecules contain both positively and negatively charged groups and are easily adsorbed by fabrics in aqueous solution. Simple salts such as sodium chloride and sodium sulfate may be added to the solution to increase the concentration of dye molecules on the fiber.
- *Substantive dyes* interact with fabrics primarily via hydrogen bonding between electron donating nitrogen atoms (–N:) in the dye and polar –OH or –CONH– groups in the fabric.

The structures of the fabric and dye molecules may be intimidating to students who are used to working with small molecules. Help students focus on ionic and polar groups in the structures—these are the groups that will influence the dyeability of a fabric. Use Question #3 in the Pre-Lab Questions *to rank the fabric molecules from most polar to least polar.*

Teacher Notes

- The ability of a dye to bond to a fabric may be improved by using an additive called a mordant. *Mordant dyes* are used in combination with salts of metal ions, typically aluminum, chromium, iron, and tin. The metal ions adhere to the fabric and serve as points of attachment for the dye molecules.

- *Vat dyes* are colored organic compounds that do not dissolve in water. Vat dyes can be reduced chemically to form colorless, water-soluble derivatives. Upon exposure to air the colorless form of a vat dye is oxidized back to the colored form. Vat dyes are introduced to the fabric in their colorless, reduced form and then "developed" by exposing the fabric with the ingrained dye to air. The most famous vat dye is indigo, which is used to dye blue jeans.

Experiment Overview

The purpose of this activity is to investigate the interaction of dyes with different fabrics. The dyes include methyl orange, malachite green, and crystal violet (direct dyes); congo red (a substantive dye); alizarin (a mordant dye); and indigo (a vat dye). See Figure 2 for the structures of the dye molecules. The dyes will be tested on a multifiber test fabric that contains strips of six different fibers—wool, acrylic, polyester, nylon, cotton, and acetate (Figure 3).

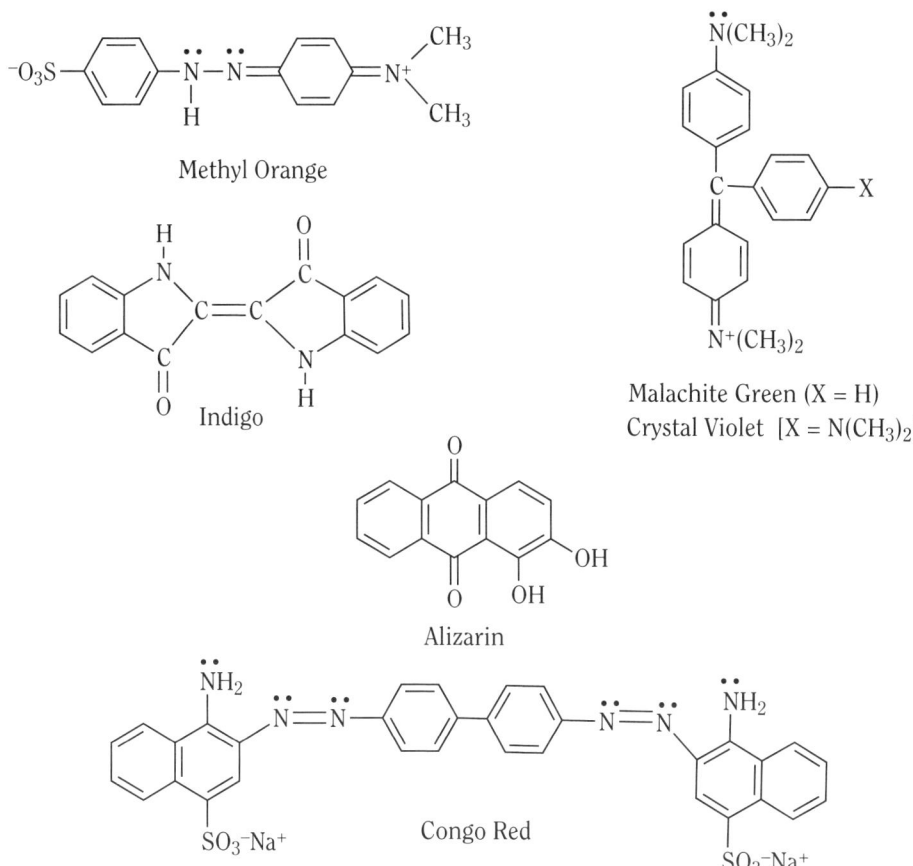

Figure 2. Chemical Structures of Dye Molecules.

Not all vat dyes are colorless in their reduced forms. Indigo, for example, is dark blue in its oxidized form, pale yellow in its reduced form.

The Color of Chemistry – Page 4

Pre-Lab Questions   Teacher Notes

1. Redraw the structure of methyl orange (Figure 2), and identify the groups in the dye that will bind to ionic and polar sites in a fabric.

2. Complete the following "If/then" hypothesis to explain how the structure of a fabric will influence the relative color intensity produced by methyl orange.

   "If a fabric contains more ionic and polar groups in its structure, then the intensity of the dye color due to methyl orange should (increase/decrease), because _____
   _____."

3. Using this hypothesis, predict the relative color intensity that will be produced by methyl orange on the six fibers in the multifiber test fabric. Rank the fabrics from 1 = lightest color to 6 = darkest color.

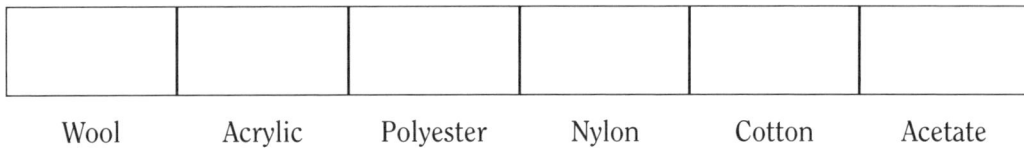

   Wool   Acrylic   Polyester   Nylon   Cotton   Acetate

   Figure 3. Composition of the Multifiber Test Fabric.

4. Form a working group with two or three other students. Read the entire *Procedure* and the recommended *Safety Precautions*. This is a cooperative lab activity—decide how you will divide up the lab work and write out an action plan. You will not have time to complete the activity if one of the partners does all the work.

Materials

Distilled water and wash bottle	***Dye baths***
Forceps or tongs	Alizarin red
Multifiber test fabric, 14 cm	Congo red
Pencil	Crystal violet
Permanent marker	Indigo
Scissors	Malachite green
Stirring rods	Methyl orange
Weighing dishes, large, 7	***Mordant bath***
Paper towels	Aluminum potassium sulfate, $AlK(SO_4)_2$

Safety Precautions

All of the dyes are strong stains and will stain skin and clothing. Methyl orange, crystal violet, and malachite green are toxic by ingestion and irritating to body tissue. Alizarin red is a body tissue irritant. The dye baths are very hot, near boiling. Exercise care to avoid scalding and skin burns. Avoid contact of all chemicals with eyes and skin. Wear chemical splash goggles and chemical-resistant gloves and apron. Wash hands thoroughly with soap and water before leaving the lab.

Page 5 – **The Color of Chemistry**

Teacher Notes

Procedure

1. Cut the multifiber test fabric crosswise to obtain seven 2-cm strips with all six fabrics on each swatch (Figure 3). Note that the wool fabric is cream-colored, not white. Use a pencil to mark the wool ends with a "W." Label the strips with your initials as well.

2. Label six weighing dishes with the names of the dyes to be tested (see the "Dye baths" in the *Materials* section). Label a seventh weighing dish "Alizarin + Alum."

3. All of the dyes are strong stains. Avoid getting any dye solution on your skin, clothes or books. To avoid contamination, rinse tongs or forceps with water before inserting them into a dye bath.

Part A. Direct Dyes

4. Fold a multifiber test strip in half. Using forceps or tongs, immerse the test strip into the *crystal violet* dye bath. *Caution:* The dye baths are very hot. Exercise care to avoid scalding or skin burns.

5. After 5–10 minutes, remove the dyed test strip from the bath using forceps. Hold the fabric above the dye bath for a few minutes and allow the excess dye solution to drain back into the dye bath.

6. Pat the test strip with paper towels and rinse the dyed test strip under running water from the faucet or a wash bottle. Continue rinsing the test strip until all of the excess dye has been removed and the rinse water is colorless.

7. Place the rinsed test strip in the appropriately labeled weighing dish and allow it to air dry.

8. Repeat steps 4–7 with new test strips in the *malachite green* and *methyl orange* dye baths.

9. When the fabrics are dry, record the dye color produced by each direct dye on each type of fabric. See the *Data Table*.

10. *(Optional)* Test whether the dyed fabrics are colorfast: Cut the dyed test strips in half to obtain two identical *1-cm strips* of dyed multifiber fabrics. Wash one test strip with soap and water and rinse well. Keep the other strip as a control. Record any color changes or observations on the data sheet.

Part B. Substantive Dye

11. Repeat steps 4–7 and 9–10 with a new multifiber test strip in the *congo red* dye bath.

Part C. Mordant Dye

Hair dryers or infrared lamps may be used to facilitate drying (step 7) in one lab period, if desired. This is not really necessary, however, because the strips will dry nicely overnight in air.

12. Use a pencil to write "Alum" on the side (selvage) of a test strip.

13. Using forceps or tongs, immerse the "alum"-labeled test strip into the boiling *mordant* bath (aluminum potassium sulfate).

14. After 15–20 minutes, remove the test strip from the mordant bath. Allow the fabric to cool slightly and then wring it out over the bath to remove excess liquid.

The Color of Chemistry

The Color of Chemistry – Page 6

15. Immerse both the mordanted test strip and an untreated test strip in the *alizarin* dye bath.

16. After 5–10 minutes, remove the test strips from the dye bath. Rinse and dry the test strips as described in Part A, steps 5–7.

17. Record the colors produced by alizarin on both the mordanted and untreated test strips.

Part D. Vat Dye

18. Immerse a test strip in the *indigo* dye bath and boil gently for 5–10 minutes.

19. Using forceps or tongs, remove the dyed test strip from the dye bath and rinse well with water.

20. Allow the test strip to air dry, then record the colors produced by indigo dyeing on each type of fabric.

Teacher Notes

Teacher Notes

Name: _____

Class/Lab Period: _____

The Color of Chemistry

Data Table

	Wool	Acrylic	Polyester	Nylon	Cotton	Acetate
Methyl Orange						
Malachite Green						
Crystal Violet						
Congo Red						
Alizarin						
Alizarin + Alum						
Indigo						
	Wool	Acrylic	Polyester	Nylon	Cotton	Acetate

(Optional) Use this space to write down any observations concerning the colorfastness of the dyes.

The Color of Chemistry – Page 8

Post-Lab Questions *(Use a separate sheet of paper to answer the following questions.)*

1. Describe the colors produced by methyl orange on the different fabrics in the multifiber test fabric. Compare the results with the relative color intensities predicted in the *Pre-Lab Questions*. Explain any differences between the predicted and actual results.

2. Compare the general ease of dyeing the six different fabrics in the multifiber test fabric. Which fabric(s) consistently developed the most intense colors, regardless of the type of dye used? Which fabric was the most difficult to dye?

3. *Consult Figure 1:* What feature stands out as unique in the structure of the fabric that was the easiest to dye? What feature stands out as unique in the structure of the fabric that was hardest to dye?

4. *Consult Figure 2:* Which two dyes have very similar structures? Compare the relative color intensities produced by these dyes on the different fabrics in the multifiber test fabric. Are the color *patterns* (from lightest to darkest) similar for these two dyes? Explain.

5. Compare the color *patterns* produced on the different types of fabrics by methyl orange (a direct dye) and congo red (a substantive dye). Suggest a possible reason for any differences based on the chemical bonding interactions of direct versus substantive dyes (see the *Background* section).

6. Show by means of a diagram one hydrogen bond that might form between a glucose unit in cotton and congo red. *Hint:* Hydrogen bonds have the general form –X–H --- :Y, where X and Y are highly electronegative atoms such as N, O, F, and Y has an unshared pair of electrons.

7. Compare the colors produced by alizarin on the untreated and mordanted test strips. What is the principal advantage of using a mordant? What fabric was almost impossible to dye except with a mordant?

Teacher Notes

Teacher's Notes
The Chemistry of Color

Master Materials List *(for a class of 30 students working in groups of three)*

Distilled water and wash bottles, 30	**Dye baths (2 each)***
Forceps or tongs, 30	Alizarin red
Multifiber test fabric, 14 cm strips, 10	Congo red
Pencils, 10	Crystal violet
Permanent markers, 10	Indigo
Scissors, 10	Malachite green
Stirring rods, 10	Methyl orange
Weighing dishes, large, 70	**Mordant bath***
Hot plates, 7†	Aluminum potassium sulfate, $AlK(SO_4)_2$
Beakers, 400-mL, 13†	Paper towels
Beakers, 1000-mL, 7*	Colored pencils (optional)

*See the *Preparation of Solutions* section.

†To ease congestion and improve safety, set up several dyeing stations around the lab. We recommend using 200 mL of dye solution in 400-mL beakers for each dye bath. To achieve even dyeing of fabrics, it is best not to immerse more than three pieces of fabric in any one dye bath at the same time. Large (7″ × 7″) hot plates will accommodate two 400-mL dye baths.

Preparation of Solutions *(for a class of 30 students working in groups of three)*

Directions are given for preparing 600 mL of each dye or mordant solution, enough for three dye baths. Dye baths may be used continuously during the day by several class sections.

Alizarin Red: Dissolve 0.8 g of alizarin in 600 mL of distilled or deionized water. Place a boiling stone in the dye solution and heat to near boiling on a hot plate.

Aluminum Potassium Sulfate (Alum): Dissolve 2.0 g of alum $[AlK(SO_4)_2]$ in 600 mL of distilled or deionized water and add 1.0 g of calcium oxide. Place a boiling stone in the solution and heat to near boiling on a hot plate.

Congo Red: Dissolve 0.2 g of congo red in 600 mL boiling water. Add 6.0 g of sodium sulfate decahydrate ($Na_2SO_4 \cdot 10H_2O$) and 4.0 g of anhydrous sodium carbonate (Na_2CO_3).

Crystal Violet: Dissolve 0.3 g of crystal violet in 600 mL of distilled or deionized water. Place a boiling stone in the dye solution and heat to near boiling on a hot plate.

Indigo: Add 1.2 g of indigo to 600 mL of water, followed by 6 mL of 3 M sodium hydroxide solution and about 6.0 g of sodium dithionite ($Na_2S_2O_4$). Place a boiling stone in the mixture and heat to boiling until the dye is reduced. This will be obvious by a color change to yellow-green and the disappearance of the insoluble indigo dye. The solution will be blue at the surface where it is exposed to the air. Cover the beaker with a watch glass to keep the blue color to a minimum. *Notes:* Sodium dithionite is also known as sodium hydrosulfite. Set up the indigo dye baths in the hood if possible. The odor of oxidized sulfur compounds, such as sulfur dioxide, may be irritating.

Teacher's Notes

Malachite Green: Dissolve 0.3 g of malachite green in 600 mL of distilled or deionized water. Place a boiling stone in the dye solution and heat to near boiling on a hot plate.

Methyl Orange: Dissolve 2.0 g of methyl orange in 600 mL of distilled or deionized water. Add 3 g of anhydrous sodium sulfate (Na_2SO_4) and 6–8 drops of concentrated sulfuric acid. Place a boiling stone in the dye solution and heat to near boiling on a hot plate.

Safety Precautions

All of the dyes are strong stains and will stain skin and clothing. Methyl orange, crystal violet, and malachite green are toxic by ingestion and irritating to body tissue. Alizarin red is a body tissue irritant. The dye baths are very hot, near boiling. Exercise care to avoid scalding and skin burns. Avoid contact of all chemicals with eyes and skin. Wear chemical splash goggles and chemical-resistant gloves and apron. Please consult current Material Safety Data Sheets for additional safety, handling, and disposal information. Remind students to wash their hands thoroughly with soap and water before leaving the lab.

Disposal

Consult your current *Flinn Scientific Catalog/Reference Manual* for general guidelines and specific procedures governing the disposal of laboratory waste. The dye solutions may be washed down the drain with plenty of excess water according to Flinn Suggested Disposal Method #26b.

Lab Hints

- The laboratory work for this activity can be completed in a typical 50-minute lab period if students work collaboratively as described in the *Pre-Lab Questions*. The experiment is far too long for completion if only one student does the actual lab work and the others merely observe or record results. Students should work on different parts of the procedure and then share results to complete the data table and answer the *Post-Lab Questions*. If three students are working together in a group, for example, each student might be responsible for testing two dyes. For best results, allow the fabrics to dry overnight before recording the final results. Students may test the colorfastness of the dyed fabrics at home, if desired.

- Place lots of paper towels or absorbent lab mats all around the dye baths. This will help keep the room clean. Instruct students to store books, bags, and other personal items away from the lab area to avoid staining them.

- The multifiber test fabric (Catalog No. AP6135) is fairly expensive but the color patterns are beautiful and intriguing. To save money, the teacher may wish to dye the multifiber test strips as part of a demonstration and have students bring fabrics of their own choosing to dye during the experiment. Suitable fabrics from home include cotton T-shirts, acrylic socks or yarn, polyester sheets, etc. Scavenge fabric stores for inexpensive bolts of white cloth (read the labels!). Pure (100%) white cotton, polyester, acetate, and nylon are easy to find and relatively inexpensive. Wash fabrics before dyeing to remove sizing and other fabric finishes.

- Other multifiber test fabrics containing 8 or 13 different fabrics are available from Testfabrics, Inc. See their Web site at www.testfabrics.com.

Teacher Notes

- Congo red is an acid–base indicator. The red color of fabrics dyed with congo red will turn blue when placed in a mild acid solution, such as 0.1 M HCl. The blue color disappears and the red color returns when the congo red–dyed fabric is placed in a washing soda bath.

- Alizarin is not the only mordant dye used in this activity. Both malachite green and crystal violet are often paired with tannic acid as a mordant for difficult-to-dye fabrics. The toxic heavy metal salt antimony potassium tartrate is required as an adjunct to "fix" the tannic acid to the fabric. Since using antimony in the lab would necessitate dedicated heavy metal waste disposal, the use of tannic acid as a mordant was omitted from this experiment. Fabrics mordanted with tannic acid must be thoroughly dried before dyeing.

- Students may experiment with other metal salts as mordants for alizarin—some interesting color changes result. Using ferrous sulfate as the mordant imparts a rich brown color to the dyed fabric.

Teaching Tips

- The "Mystery Nylon Factory" demonstration kit available from Flinn Scientific (Catalog No. AP2088) provides a good lead-in to this activity. Use the nylon rope trick demonstration to introduce the idea of polymers and talk about their unique characteristics. One point worth mentioning is that individual polymer molecules do not all have the same molecular weight. Polymers are polydisperse—the molecular weight is an average based on the number of molecules having different molecular weights in a sample (the so-called number-average molecular weight).

- The history and chemistry of dyeing with indigo are explored in greater detail in "Dyeing with Indigo," a student laboratory kit available from Flinn Scientific (Catalog No. AP6166).

Teacher's Notes

Answers to Pre-Lab Questions *(Student answers will vary.)*

1. Redraw the structure of methyl orange (Figure 2), and identify the groups in the dye that will bind to ionic and polar sites in a fabric.

   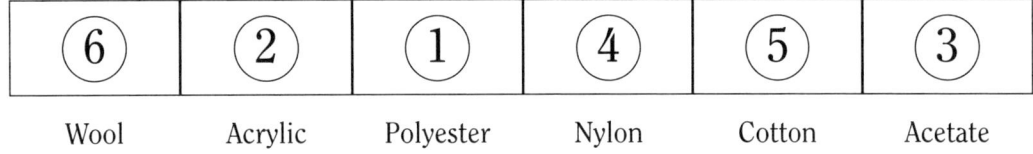

   Binds to polar and ionic sites   *Binds to polar sites*   *Binds to ionic sites*

2. Complete the following "If/then" hypothesis to explain how the structure of a fabric will influence the relative color intensity produced by methyl orange.

   "If a fabric contains more ionic and polar groups in its structure, then the intensity of the dye color due to methyl orange should *increase,* because *there will be more sites on the fabric for the dye molecules to bind to."*

3. Using this hypothesis, predict the relative color intensity that will be produced by methyl orange on the six fibers in the multifiber test fabric. Rank the fabrics from 1 = lightest color to 6 = darkest color.

6	2	1	4	5	3
Wool	Acrylic	Polyester	Nylon	Cotton	Acetate

   Figure 3. Composition of the Multifiber Test Fabric.

   Note to teachers: *Ask students to arrange the fabric molecules from least polar to most polar. See the* Background *section.*

4. Form a working group with two or three other students. Read the entire *Procedure* and the recommended *Safety Precautions*. This is a cooperative lab activity—decide how you will divide up the lab work and write out an action plan. You will not have time to complete the activity if one of the partners does all the work.

   Note to teachers: *Ask to see the students' plans!*

Teacher's Notes

Teacher Notes

Sample Data

Student data will vary.

Data Table

	Wool	Acrylic	Polyester	Nylon	Cotton	Acetate
Methyl Orange	Red	White	Pale yellow	Orange	Light yellow	Yellow
Malachite Green	Dark green	Blue-green	Pale green	Light green	Blue-green	Turquoise
Crystal Violet	Dark blue	Periwinkle	Light blue	Blue	Royal blue	Blue
Congo Red	Red	Pink	Light pink	Red	Dark red	Red
Alizarin	Violet	Pale pink	Pink	Lavender	Mauve	Cream
Alizarin + Alum	Dark purple	Purple	Purple	Purple	Purple	Purple
Indigo	Navy blue*	Light blue	Light blue	Navy blue	Blue	Navy blue
	Wool	Acrylic	Polyester	Nylon	Cotton	Acetate

*The wool fiber appeared to disintegrate in the basic vat dye bath used for indigo.

(*Optional*) Use this space to write down any observations concerning the colorfastness of the dyes.

All of the dyes were colorfast. There were a few exceptions:

- *The color of malachite green on cotton faded after washing.*
- *The color of crystal violet on both cotton and polyester also faded after washing.*

See the back inside cover for color photographs of the dyed test fabrics.

The Color of Chemistry

Teacher's Notes

Answers to Post-Lab Questions *(Student answers will vary.)*

1. Describe the colors produced by methyl orange on the different fabrics in the multifiber test fabric. Compare the results with the relative color intensities predicted in the *Pre-Lab Questions*. Explain any differences between the predicted and actual results.

   Observed color intensity:

   Wool > nylon > acetate > cotton > polyester > acrylic

   The color of methyl orange ranged from dark red-orange on wool and bright orange on nylon to essentially colorless (white) on acrylic. Acetate was dyed lemon yellow, while cotton and polyester were light yellow and pale yellow, respectively.
   Note to teachers: *Student predictions in the* Pre-Lab Questions *will vary. Most should predict that wool will show the greatest affinity for the dye, and thus the most intense color with methyl orange. The results for nylon may be a surprise, since there are no charged groups shown in the structure of nylon. Students may notice, however, that both nylon and wool contain amide-linking groups in their repeating units—maybe the polar amide groups interact very strongly with the dye via hydrogen bonding.*

2. Compare the general ease of dyeing the six different fabrics in the multifiber test fabric. Which fabric(s) consistently developed the most intense colors, regardless of the type of dye used? Which fabric was the most difficult to dye?

   Wool consistently developed the most intense colors with all of the dyes except congo red. Even with congo red, however, wool was only a shade paler than cotton, which gave the most intense color. Nylon, cotton, and acetate were also relatively easy to dye. They gave fairly intense colors with at least four out of the six dyes tested. Polyester was the most difficult fabric to dye.

3. *Consult Figure 1:* What feature stands out as unique in the structure of the fabric that was the easiest to dye? What feature stands out as unique in the structure of the fabric that was hardest to dye?

   Wool contains many charged groups in its structure. None of the other fabrics show any charged groups in their normal repeating units. Polyester is unique in that it appears to be the least polar of all the fabrics. Polyester has no –X–H (where X = O or N) groups capable of forming hydrogen bonds with electron donor sites in dye molecules. ***Note to teachers:*** *Students may notice that acrylic fiber is similar to polyester in that is lacks polar groups capable of hydrogen bonding to electron donor sites in dye molecules. The dyeability of acrylic is improved commercially by incorporating small amounts of charged monomers such as AMPS (see below) into the growing polymer.*

$$CH_2=CH-\overset{\overset{O}{\|}}{C}-NH-CH_2-C(CH_3)_2-SO_3^{\ominus}$$

Structure of AMPS

Teacher's Notes

Teacher Notes

4. *Consult Figure 2:* Which two dyes have very similar structures? Compare the relative color intensities produced by these dyes on the different fabrics in the multifiber test fabric. Are the color *patterns* (from lightest to darkest) similar for these two dyes? Explain.

   Crystal violet and malachite green have similar structures and produced similar color patterns with the six fabrics in the multifiber test fabric. The observed color intensity produced by crystal violet and malachite green was:

   Wool > cotton, acrylic, and acetate > nylon >> polyester.

5. Compare the color *patterns* produced on the different types of fabrics by methyl orange (a direct dye) and congo red (a substantive dye). Suggest a possible reason for any differences based on the chemical bonding interactions of direct versus substantive dyes (see the *Background* section).

   Congo red dyed every fabric! It gave nice bright reds of almost equal color intensity with four of the fabrics (wool, nylon, cotton, and acetate) and light pink colors with acrylic and polyester. Methyl orange showed a much greater variability in the colors that it produced on different fabrics (see Question #1). Binding of methyl orange may depend on its ability to form ionic bonds with fabric molecules. Congo red binds to fabrics via hydrogen bonding. More fabrics are capable of hydrogen bonding than ionic bonding.

6. Show by means of a diagram one hydrogen bond that might form between a glucose unit in cotton and congo red. *Hint:* Hydrogen bonds have the general form –X–H --- :Y, where X and Y are highly electronegative atoms such as N, O, F, and Y has an unshared pair of electrons.

7. Compare the colors produced by alizarin on the untreated and mordanted test strips. What is the principal advantage of using a mordant? What fabric was almost impossible to dye except with a mordant?

   The effect of the mordant was unique—it produced almost equal color intensity (shades of purple) on every fabric in the multifiber test fabric. The untreated test strip showed large variations in the color shade produced with alizarin. The mordanted test strip was simply purple almost all the way across. The only exception was wool, which was darker than the rest of the fabrics on the mordanted test strip. The effect of the mordant was most significant on polyester, which was almost impossible to dye using any other dyes.

The Color of Chemistry

Teacher's Notes

Demonstrations

Teacher Notes

Go Fish for an Ion
A Chemistry Card Game

Introduction
Review the names and charges of common ions and learn the chemical formulas of ionic compounds while having fun with this engaging chemistry card game.

Concepts
- Ionic compounds
- Cations and anions
- Empirical formulas
- Ion charges

Materials *(for a class of 24 students playing in groups of four)*
Go Fish for an Ion Playing Cards, 6 decks (64 cards per deck)
Go Fish for an Ion List of Ion Cards, 6
Go Fish for an Ion Score Sheets, 24

Preparation

1. Use the following template to design copy masters of *Go Fish for an Ion* playing cards.

2. Use the information in Table 1 to prepare cards for the ions listed. There are 10 cations, 10 anions, and 64 cards total. The number of cards for each ion and their assigned point values are shown in the table.

3. Make one copy of the "Rules of the Game" for each player.

4. Make one copy of the "Score Sheet" for each player.

5. Make enough copies of the "List of Ion Cards" (Table 1) so that each playing group of four students may have a copy at the playing table.

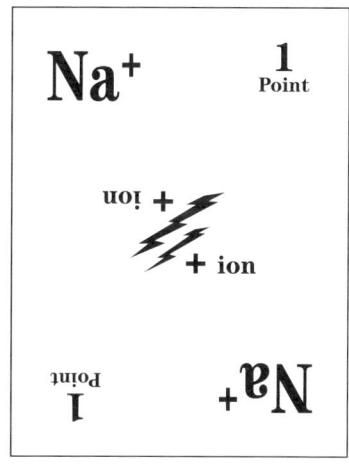

Tips

- Use an overhead projector to demonstrate an acceptable match and an unacceptable match to the students.

- Consider laminating the "Rules of the Game," "Score Sheet," and the playing cards to extend their useful life.

- "Go Fish for an Ion" is an excellent practice or review activity for students to play during the unit or prior to a test. Completed score sheets list cations, anions, and the formulas of compounds and thus make good study guides.

Special thanks to Laura Spencer, Edmonds–Woodway High School, Edmonds WA, for providing the idea and instructions for this activity. "Go Fish for an Ion" is available as a student activity kit from Flinn Scientific (Catalog No. AP6131).

Demonstrations

Table 1. List of Ion Cards

Cations

Symbol	Name	Points	# of Cards
Li^+	Lithium	1	6
K^+	Potassium	1	6
Na^+	Sodium	1	6
NH_4^+	Ammonium	2	4
Cu^+	Cuprous	2	2
Fe^{2+}	Ferrous	2	2
Ca^{2+}	Calcium	3	4
Cu^{2+}	Cupric	3	2
Fe^{3+}	Ferric	4	2
Al^{3+}	Aluminum	6	2

Anions

Symbol	Name	Points	# of Cards
Cl^-	Chloride	1	2
OH^-	Hydroxide	2	2
NO_3^-	Nitrate	2	3
NO_2^-	Nitrite	2	3
O^{2-}	Oxide	3	3
S^{2-}	Sulfide	3	3
CO_3^{2-}	Carbonate	4	3
SO_4^{2-}	Sulfate	4	3
SO_3^{2-}	Sulfite	4	3
PO_4^{3-}	Phosphate	6	3

Teacher Notes

Two methods are used for naming cations with more than one common ionic charge. The Latin-based classical naming system uses the suffix -ous attached to the root name of the metal to indicate the cation having the lower of two possible ionic charges. The suffix -ic is used in this system to denote the cation having the higher of two possible ionic charges. In the Roman numeral–based stock system, a Roman numeral in parentheses is used to denote the positive charge on the cation. Thus, the cuprous ion (Table 1) is also called the copper(I) cation, and the cupric ion is also called the copper(II) cation.

Demonstrations

Teacher Notes

Go Fish for an Ion
The Rules of the Game

Number of Players—Four to five players are recommended.

Duration of Game—Thirty minutes is a reasonable game time. Consider setting a timer and calling the game when the timer goes off.

Getting Started—Dealer deals out seven cards to each player and scatters the remaining cards face down in the middle of the table. This is the "Fishing Pond." Each player should have a *Score Sheet*. There should be at least one *List of Ion Cards* sheet setting out for players to check what ions are available.

Matches—Game play begins clockwise from the dealer. Player 1 lays down (face up) any matches in hand at this time that will make a compound (see the *How to Make a Match* section). The player records on the score sheet the cation, the anion, the number of each ion needed to form a neutral ionic compound, and the chemical formula. Other players check that the match is appropriate and verify the formula. The teacher should be available to arbitrate disputes.

How to Make a Match—Each match must have the correct number of cations (+) and anions (–) to balance their charges and form a neutral compound. To simplify the game, consider only one type of cation and one type of anion per match.

Acceptable Matches			*Unacceptable Matches*		
Na^+	Na^+	SO_4^{2-}	Li^+	Na^+	SO_4^{2-}
Al^{3+}	Cl^-	Cl^- Cl^-	Al^{3+}	O^{2-}	
K^+	K^+	S^{2-}	NH_4^+	PO_4^{3-}	

Trading—After laying down all matches currently in hand, Player 1 determines which cards may be needed to make a match. To do this, Player 1 may examine the *List of Ion Cards* to see which ions are available in the deck and which have already been laid down (face up) on the table. Player 1 then asks of a *specific* player "Do you have a *(blank)* ion?"

The Player who has has been asked must give ALL cards for this ion to Player 1 and then replenishes his/her hand by drawing cards from the "Fishing Pond." Player 1 may now lay down a match, if possible, and the turn is over.

If the player does not have the requested ion, he tells Player 1 to "Go Fish" for the ion. Player 1 draws a card from the "Fishing Pond" and the turn is over. Play then continues with the next player in a clockwise rotation. *Note:* A match may not be laid down until the next turn.

Points—Each card is worth a specified point value. To determine points for a correct match, the player adds up the points for all the cards in the match and records the score on the score sheet. Both the match *and* the formula must be correct to score points. *Bonus points* may be awarded if a player matches up all of his/her cards. This can be a fairly frequent occurrence. That player earns 10 bonus points, may draw 7 new cards from the "Fishing Pond," and the turn is over. Point values are based on the frequency of card appearance in the deck.

The rules of the game may be extended to include the names of the ionic compounds formed in the matches. Add a column "Name" to the score sheet and assign points for a correctly named compound.

Go Fish for an Ion

Demonstrations

Name: _____

Class/Lab Period: _____

Go Fish for an Ion
Score Sheet

Cation	# Cations	Anion	# of Anions	Chemical Formula	Points
Ex: Cu^{2+}	1	OH^-	2	$Cu(OH)_2$	(2 pts)(1) + (2 pts)(2) = 6

Teacher Notes

Teacher Notes

Electronegativity
A Simple Demonstration Device

Introduction

Help students visualize the abstract concept of electronegativity and its significance in polar and nonpolar covalent bonding with this inexpensive and easy-to-make demonstration device.

Concepts

- Covalent bonding
- Nonpolar vs. polar bonds
- Electronegativity
- Bonding electron pair

Materials

Rubber bands of equal length but different elasticities (thicknesses), 2
Rubber bands of equal length and the same elasticities (thicknesses), 2
Paper clips, large (5-cm length), 4
Ring stands, 2 (optional)
Styrofoam® balls (1.5″ or 3.8-cm diameter), 4
Knife

Safety Precautions

Although the materials used in this demonstration are considered nonhazardous, please observe all normal laboratory safety guidelines. Take care to avoid possible injury due to "accidental" misuse of rubber bands.

Procedure

Part A. Polar Covalent Bond Model

1. Link two paper clips together in end-to-end fashion to make a "chain" as shown in Figure 1.

2. Loop one strong (thick) rubber band through the outer end of one of the paper clips.

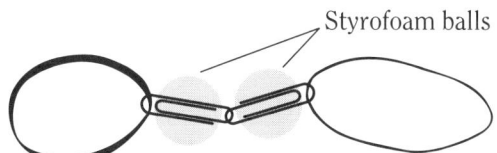

Figure 1. Polar Covalent Bonding Device.

3. Loop one weak (thin) rubber band through the outer end of the other paper clip. The two rubber bands should be on opposite ends of the paper clip chain.

4. Use a knife to carefully make a slit halfway through each Styrofoam ball. (Slice the ball as if you were going to cut the ball in half, but stop at the center of the ball.) Then slide these "electron" balls over the paper clips as shown in Figure 1.

5. Grasp the rubber bands, one in each hand, and slowly pull the device apart. Observe that the two Styrofoam balls—the bonding pair of electrons—are much closer spatially to the hand holding the thicker rubber band.

Special thanks to Jeffrey D. Bracken, Westerville High School, Westerville OH, for bringing this idea to our attention.

Demonstrations

Part B. Nonpolar Covalent Bond Model

6. The nonpolar covalent bonding model is almost identical to the polar covalent model except for the choice of rubber bands—the two rubber bands used in the nonpolar covalent bond model should have the same elasticity.

7. When this model is stretched, the two electrons remain equidistant from both atoms. This illustrates that the two atoms share the two bonding electrons equally between them.

Tip

- The two rubber bands of the models may be looped over ring stands as shown in Figure 2. The ring stands should be anchored to the benchtop to keep the rubber bands taut and to prevent the stands from tipping over. Stacking textbooks on the base may help anchor the ring stands. Using the ring stands allows teachers to keep their hands free during the discussion without having to remove the model from the students' view. If desired, elemental symbols can be drawn on construction paper and taped to the ring stands.

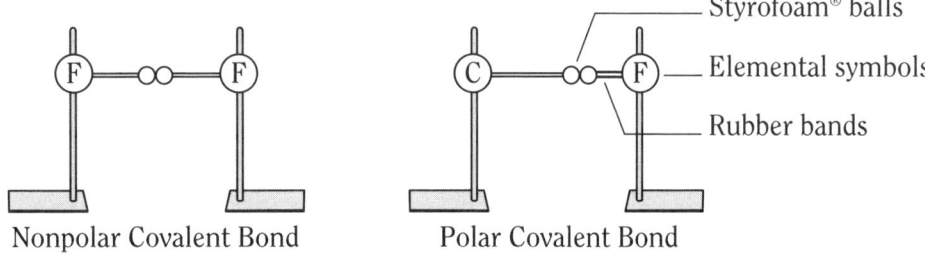

Nonpolar Covalent Bond Polar Covalent Bond

Figure 2. Comparison of Nonpolar and Polar Covalent Bonds.

Discussion

Many chemistry students experience difficulty understanding the abstract concept of electronegativity and its significance in polar versus nonpolar covalent bonding. The popular use of Pauling electronegativity series in many general chemistry textbooks allows students to identify nonpolar covalent, polar covalent, and ionic bonds based on the electronegativity difference of the two atoms involved in the bond. While this approach may be successful in a quantitative manner, it does not help students recognize the origin or nature of electronegativity.

The effectiveness of concrete models during the initial stages of instruction is appreciated by teachers at all levels. In an effort to help students "see" the concept of electronegativity, a simple, inexpensive model has been created—one that will provide students with a visual representation of electronegativity.

While introducing the concept of electronegativity to students, it is common to describe covalent bonding as a "tug-of-war" for electrons. Continuing with this analogy, this demonstration can be set up by saying that each hand represents an atom, and that each atom exerts a force and pulls on the shared pair of electrons. The students can then be asked to predict which atom will possess a partial positive or partial negative charge in the resulting covalent bond model. Students often forget that electrons have a negative charge and thus find the assignment of partial charges confusing.

Teacher Notes

Teacher Notes

Splatter Test
Properties of Liquids Demonstration

Introduction

The properties of liquids reflect the bonding within molecules and the nature and strength of forces between molecules. The rate of evaporation of different liquids is a good starting point to introduce the forces between molecules that influence vapor pressure and boiling point.

Concepts

- Intermolecular forces
- Hydrogen bonding
- Dipole–dipole interactions
- London dispersion forces

Materials

Water, H_2O, 5 mL

Acetone, C_3H_6O, 5 mL

Ethyl alcohol, C_2H_6O, 5 mL

Beral-type pipets, 3

Safety Precautions

Acetone and ethyl alcohol are flammable liquids; keep away from flames, heat, and other sources of ignition. The solvents are slightly toxic by ingestion and inhalation. Perform this demonstration in a well-ventilated room. Wear chemical splash goggles and chemical-resistant gloves and apron. Please review current Material Safety Data Sheets for additional safety, handling, and disposal information.

Procedure

1. Draw the structures of acetone, ethyl alcohol, and water on a classroom board.

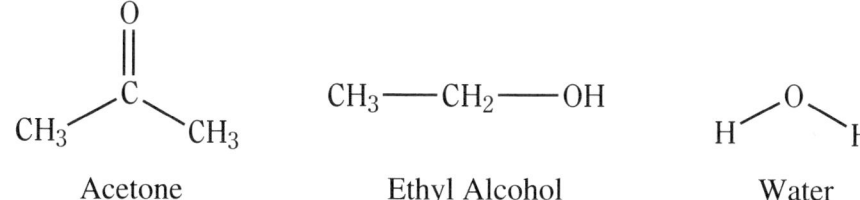

      Acetone   Ethyl Alcohol   Water

2. Enlist volunteers to help with the demonstration. Steps 3–5 should be done simultaneously.

3. Squirt several milliliters of water onto the classroom board under the structure of water.

4. Squirt several milliliters of ethyl alcohol onto the classroom board under the structure of ethyl alcohol.

5. Squirt several milliliters of acetone onto the classroom board under the structure of acetone.

6. Observe the rate of spreading of the liquids on the surface of the board and the rate of evaporation of the liquids.

Disposal

None required.

Splatter Test

Demonstrations

Tips

Teacher Notes

- A less spectacular version of this demonstration uses cotton balls soaked in solvent and rubbed on the board. This may be a good alternative if the classroom is not ventilated.

- Other solvents that may be used in this demonstration include nonpolar hydrocarbons that are more volatile than acetone, and glycerol, which is less volatile than water.

Discussion

Evaporation is the gradual change of state from liquid to gas that occurs at a liquid's surface. The rate of evaporation of a particular substance depends on the temperature, which reflects the average kinetic energy of the molecules. Differences in the evaporation rate of two liquids at the same temperature arise due to differences in the intermolecular forces holding the liquid together.

Molecules are "held together" in condensed phases (liquids and solids) by intermolecular forces. Intermolecular forces are defined as attractive forces between molecules. There are three kinds of intermolecular forces—dipole–dipole interactions, hydrogen bonds, and dispersion (London) forces. These forces vary in strength, with hydrogen bonds being the strongest and London dispersion forces the weakest.

Dipole–dipole interactions are electrostatic attractive forces between the negative end of one molecular dipole and the positive end of another dipole. These forces apply only to polar molecules.

Hydrogen bonds are a special case of dipole–dipole forces with very specific structural requirements. Hydrogen bonding always involves a hydrogen atom attached to a highly electronegative atom such as F, O, N, or Cl. This hydrogen atom is attracted to and shares electrons with an unshared pair of electrons on an electronegative atom in an adjacent molecule. For example, water molecules form a highly associated, hydrogen-bonded network in which each oxygen atom forms two strong hydrogen bonds with two hydrogen atoms in neighboring molecules (see Figure 1).

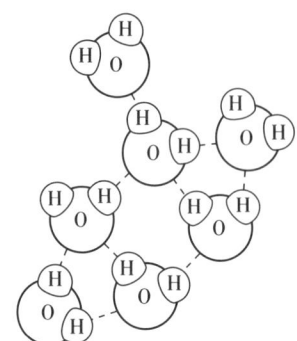

Figure 1. Hydrogen Bonding Between Water Molecules.

London dispersion forces are present between all molecules, both polar or nonpolar. Dispersion forces arise due to "induced polarization" of bonds within molecules—random, instantaneous dipoles resulting from electron motion. These weak, short-lived dipoles attract each other just as permanent dipoles do, although not as strongly.

In this demonstration, the observed rate of evaporation for the three liquids is:

Acetone > ethyl alcohol > water.

The slow rate of evaporation of water molecules reflects the strong hydrogen bonding in water—only the water molecules at the liquid surface that have enough kinetic energy to break the hydrogen bonds will escape into the gas phase. Hydrogen bonding is also present in ethyl alcohol, although to a lesser extent than in water. Acetone is a polar compound—the molecules are held together in the liquid phase by dipole–dipole forces, which are weaker than hydrogen bonds.

Flinn ChemTopic™ Labs — Chemical Bonding

Teacher Notes

Demonstrations

Graphite Disk Demonstration
Face-Up or Face-Down?

Introduction

Observe the orientation of graphite-coated paper disks in two-phase solvent systems containing water and an organic solvent. Will the graphite side of the paper disk emerge face-up or face-down in the solvent mixture? Use this demonstration to illustrate the difference between polar and nonpolar substances and their affinity for one another.

Concepts

- Covalent bonds
- Polar vs. nonpolar compounds

Materials

Food coloring (optional)
Hexane, C_6H_{14}, 50 mL
Pencil, No. 2
Trichloroethylene, C_2Cl_3H, 50 mL
Water, 100 mL

Bottles, wide-mouth, or beakers, 250-mL, 2
Graduated cylinder, 50-mL
Index card, white, 3 × 5 inches
Paper punch
Stirring rods, 2 (optional)

Safety Precautions

Trichloroethylene is a possible carcinogen. It is slightly toxic by ingestion and inhalation—the vapor may be harmful to the eyes, skin, and lungs. Avoid breathing the vapor and work with the solvent in a fume hood or well-ventilated lab only. Hexane is a flammable solvent and a dangerous fire risk; avoid contact with flames, heat, and other sources of ignition. Wear chemical splash goggles and chemical-resistant gloves and apron. Please review current Material Safety Data Sheets for additional safety, handling, and disposal information.

Procedure

1. Using a No. 2 pencil, thoroughly blacken one side only of an index card with graphite (pencil lead). Punch out 20–30 paper disks with a paper punch.

2. Add 50 mL of water and 50 mL of trichloroethylene to a wide-mouth bottle or 250-mL beaker.

3. Add about 10 graphite-coated disks to the bottle and cap the bottle, if possible.

4. Shake the bottle once (or stir the mixture in the beaker) and observe the orientation of the graphite disks in the two-phase solvent system.

5. *(Optional)* Pass the bottle around and ask students to suggest possible explanations for the observed orientation of the graphite and paper sides of the paper disks. *(The disks should all be lying with their graphite-coated sides face down toward the more dense, lower solvent layer, trichloroethylene.)*

6. Add 50 mL of water and 50 mL of hexane to a second wide-mouth bottle or 250-mL beaker.

Graphite Disk Demonstration

Demonstrations

Teacher Notes

7. Add about 10 graphite-coated disks to the bottle and cap the bottle, if possible.

8. Shake the bottle once (or stir the mixture in the beaker) and observe the orientation of the graphite disks in the two-phase solvent system.

9. *(Optional)* Pass the bottle around and ask students to suggest possible explanations for the observed orientation of the graphite and paper sides of the paper disks. *(The disks should all be lying with their graphite-coated sides face up toward the less dense, upper solvent layer, hexane.)*

10. *(Optional)* Remove 10–15 drops of each liquid layer from the two solvent systems and place them in separate test tubes. Add food coloring to determine which layer is which. *(Food dyes are ionic and highly polar compounds that are soluble in water, insoluble in nonpolar organic solvents.)*

Disposal

Consult your current *Flinn Scientific Catalog/Reference Manual* for general guidelines and specific procedures governing the disposal of laboratory waste. Remove the graphite disks from the two-phase solvent systems. Separate the two liquid layers in each bottle and save the organic solvents in properly labeled bottles for future use.

Tip

- The recommended organic solvents are trichloroethylene and "hexanes," a mixture of *n*-hexane and other C_6H_{14} isomers. Trichloroethylene is more dense than water and forms the lower layer in a two-phase solvent system with water. Hexane is less dense than water and forms the upper layer in a two-phase solvent system with water. Both solvents are nonpolar and immiscible with water. Other heavier-than-water halogenated organic solvents, such as methylene chloride or chloroform, may also be used. Take special care when using more volatile halogenated organic solvents—they have very low TLV values and may be narcotic even at low concentrations.

Discussion

Paper is made from cellulose, a polysaccharide composed of glucose repeating units. The presence of multiple –OH groups per glucose unit makes the paper surface very hydrophilic—it is attracted to water molecules. Graphite, the most stable form of the element carbon, is composed of rings of carbon atoms joined together via covalent bonds to form a layered structure. Because all of the atoms in graphite are the same, graphite is a nonpolar, hydrophobic substance. In a two-phase solvent system composed of water and a nonpolar organic solvent, the graphite disks will always orient themselves such that the paper side faces the water layer and the graphite side faces the organic solvent layer.

Teacher Notes

Demonstrations

Properties of Metals
Crystal Structure and Heat Treatment

Introduction

Heat treatment of metals is used to increase their hardness and their "workability"—their ability to be bent and shaped. Annealing, hardening, and tempering are examples of changes that occur in the properties of metals as they are heated and cooled. Models of metal crystal structure can help us visualize the changes that take place during the heat treatment of a metal.

Concepts

- Properties of metals
- Crystal structure
- Body-centered cubic
- Face-centered cubic

Materials

Bobby pins, 16
Bunsen burner
Beaker, 250-mL
Crucible tongs
Heat-resistant pad or wire gauze

Styrofoam balls, 2", 25
Chenille wires (pipe cleaners), 5-cm lengths, 25
Scissors
Water

Safety Precautions

Exercise care when working with hot metals. Wear chemical splash goggles and heat-resistant gloves whenever working with heat, chemicals or glassware in the lab.

Procedure

Part A. Heat Treatment of a Metal

1. Ask students to describe the properties of the metal in a bobby pin. Determine the average number of times a bobby pin can be bent back and forth before it will break. *(On average, a bobby pin will break after it has been straightened out and rebent seven times.)*

2. Hold the ends of a bobby pin with crucible tongs. Heat the bend of the pin in a burner flame until the metal is red hot. Place the pin on a heat-resistant surface and allow to cool to room temperature. Repeat if desired to obtain several samples for testing.

3. Test the properties of the metal: Count the number of times the treated pins can be bent back and forth before breaking. *(The treated pins are easier to bend and more difficult to break—the treated pins can be bent back and forth about 12 times before breaking.)*

4. Steps 2 and 3 represent the *annealing* process. Define annealing. *(Annealing is the process of strong heating followed by slow cooling. Annealing softens a metal and makes it less brittle.)*

5. Hold the ends of a bobby pin with crucible tongs and heat the pin in a burner flame until it is red hot. Immediately drop the pin into a beaker of cold water. Repeat if desired.

Properties of Metals

Demonstrations

6. Remove the pins from the water and dry them. Test the properties of the metal: Count the number of times the treated pins can be bent back and forth before breaking. *(The pins are extremely hard to bend and break easily—on average, the pins break on the first try!)*

7. Steps 5 and 6 represent the *hardening* process. Define hardening. *(Hardening is the process of strong heating followed by "quenching" or rapid cooling. Hardening makes a metal very rigid and brittle.)*

8. Heat a bobby pin until it is red hot, then drop it into cold water to cool it quickly. Dry the pin and *gently* reheat the pin by holding it above a burner flame until it acquires a blue oxide coating. Place the pin on a heat-resistant surface and allow to cool to room temperature. Repeat if desired.

9. Test the properties of the metal: Count the number of times the treated pins can be bent back and forth before breaking. *(The pins are hard but "springy"—they do not break.)*

10. Steps 8 and 9 represent the *tempering* process. Define tempering. *(Tempering is the process of strong heating and rapid cooling followed by gentle reheating and slow cooling. Tempering reduces the extreme hardness of the metal but increases its "toughness." The tempered metal is nonbrittle.)*

Part B. Models of BCC and FCC Crystal Structure

11. Using 5-cm chenille stems, attach four Styrofoam balls together to form a square, as shown in Figure 1a. *Note:* Leave a short, 0.5-cm space (stem) between the balls to separate them. This space is necessary for packing the balls into subsequent layers.

12. Place a single ball so that it occupies the "hole" created in the middle of the first square of balls (Figure 1b).

13. Repeat step 11 to form another layer of four balls arranged in a square. Place this layer on top of the middle ball so that the balls are aligned directly over the balls in the lowest layer, as shown in Figure 1c. This is a body-centered cubic (BCC) crystal structure.

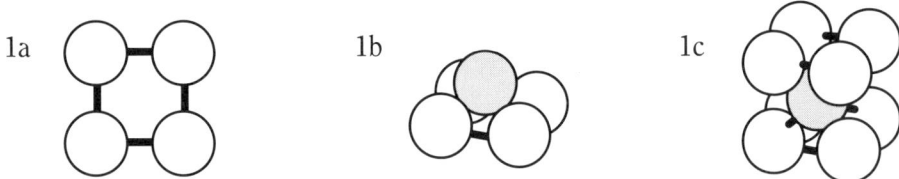

Figure 1. Body-centered Cubic Crystal Structure.

14. *(Optional)* If desired, attach the ball in the middle layer diagonally to two balls in opposite corners of the lower and upper layers to secure the BCC model.

Teacher Notes

Demonstrations

Teacher Notes

15. Examine the BCC model: Why is this arrangement of atoms called a body-centered cubic structure? How many "nearest neighbors" surround the central atom in the structure? *(The BCC structure consists of a cube with one atom in each corner or vertex of the cube and an additional atom in the center or body of the cube. The central atom has eight "nearest neighbors"—this is the "coordination number" for a metal atom in the BCC structure.)*

16. To prepare a model of a face-centered cubic (FCC) crystal structure, attach four Styrofoam balls at 90° angles to a center ball, as shown in Figure 2a. It is not necessary to leave any space or stem showing between the balls. This will be the lower layer of atoms.

17. To make the middle layer of atoms, attach four balls together to form a square (Figure 2b).

18. Repeat step 16 form another layer of five atoms. This will be the upper layer of atoms in the FCC crystal structure. Arrange the lower, middle, and upper layers together as shown in Figure 2c.

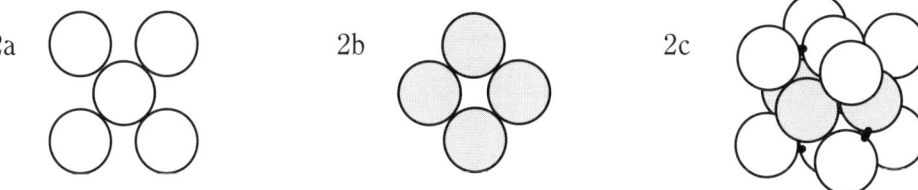

Figure 2. Face-centered Cubic Crystal Structure.

19. *(Optional)* If desired, attach one ball in each of the lower and upper layers to one ball in the middle layer to secure the FCC model.

20. Examine the FCC model: Why is this arrangement of atoms called a face-centered cubic structure? *(The FCC structure consists of a cube with one atom at each vertex of the cube and one atom in the center of each side or "face" of the cube.)*

21. *(Optional)* Repeat step 17 to construct another "middle" layer of four balls and add this to the top of the structure as a fourth layer. Count the number of balls that surround the center ball in the third layer. How many "nearest neighbors" surround this atom? *(Each atom in the FCC crystal structure is surrounded by 12 "nearest neighbors"—this is the coordination number for a metal atom in the FCC structure.)*

Disposal

Consult your current *Flinn Scientific Catalog/Reference Manual* for general guidelines and specific procedures governing the disposal of laboratory waste. Used metal pins may be disposed of in the trash according to Flinn Suggested Disposal Method #26a.

Demonstrations

Tips

- This demonstration may be carried out as a cooperative class activity. Divide the class into six groups of about four students each and have two groups perform the bobby pin experiments, two groups build the BCC model and analyze its features, and two groups build the FCC model and analyze its features. The teacher can then coordinate a class discussion in which all of the groups share their findings.

- Metals that crystallize in the BCC crystal structure include vanadium, chromium, manganese, iron, and all of the alkali metals. Metals that crystallize in the FCC crystal structure include aluminum, lead, copper, silver, and gold.

- The FCC structure is an example of "closest packing" of solids—identical atoms are packed as closely as possible into a given space. If one assumes that the atoms behave as small spheres, the atoms occupy 74% of the volume of the FCC crystal structure and have a coordination number of 12. This is the maximum coordination number and maximum density possible for atoms in a solid lattice composed of small "spheres."

- Sodium chloride crystallizes in a FCC crystal structure. To build a model of the sodium chloride crystal structure, pack one-inch Styrofoam balls into all of the spaces between the two-inch balls in the FCC model (step 18). The larger balls represent the chloride anions, the smaller balls the sodium cations.

Discussion

Bobby pins are made of steel—iron that has been alloyed with about 1% carbon to improve its hardness and toughness. Heat treatment affects the crystal structure of the metal. At room temperature, steel crystallizes in a BCC structure called *alpha*-ferrite. This BCC structure does not dissolve carbon and is soft and ductile. Heating the BCC form transforms it into a FCC crystal structure that dissolves carbon and is very hard. Sudden cooling of the high-temperature FCC structure by quenching it in water (hardening) causes the dissolved carbon atoms to become trapped in the BCC lattice. The resulting stress and distortions in the crystal structure make the metal extremely hard but also very brittle. This form of iron is called martensite. Slow cooling of the high-temperature FCC structure (annealing) allows the iron to crystallize in the stable BCC form and the carbon to precipitate out in the form of large particles that cause minimal disruption or dislocation of the crystal structure. The result is a soft, nonbrittle, very workable form of the metal. Gentle reheating of the hardened form followed by slow cooling (tempering) allows the trapped carbon to precipitate and removes many of the internal stresses in the distorted martensite crystal structure. This reduces the extreme hardness of the metal but also eliminates the brittleness. The tempered metal is very strong yet still "workable."

Demonstrations

Teacher Notes

Super Duper Polymer
Polyethylene Oxide Demonstration

Introduction

A super duper polymer gel will climb up and out the side of the beaker against the force of gravity in this demonstration of polymer properties and hydrogen bonding.

Concepts

- Polymers
- Viscosity
- Hydrogen bonding
- Bond lengths and bond angles

Materials

Methyl or ethyl alcohol, 25 mL
Polyethylene oxide, 3–4 g
Fluorescent dye, fluorescein or rhodamine B (optional)

Graduated cylinder, 25-mL
Beaker, 600-mL, 2
Stirring rod
Food dye (optional)

Safety Precautions

Methyl alcohol is a flammable solvent and dangerous fire risk. It is toxic by ingestion. Keep away from flames and other sources of ignition. Wear chemical splash goggles and chemical-resistant gloves and apron. Please review current Material Safety Data Sheets for additional safety, handling, and disposal information.

Procedure

1. Mix 20–25 mL of an anhydrous alcohol such as methyl or ethyl alcohol with 3–4 grams of polyethylene oxide in a clean, dry 600-mL beaker. Swirl the mixture to completely wet the resin with alcohol. The polymer will not dissolve, but will be a free-flowing slurry.

2. Add 350–400 mL of tap water into the alcohol–polymer mixture "in one pour". Use a stirring rod to stir the mixture until the polymer has dissolved and the solution is homogeneous and thick.

3. Pour the gel into a second 600-mL beaker and then pour back and forth between the two beakers to finish mixing the gel.

4. The polyethylene oxide can be made to siphon "uphill" out of a beaker and against gravity. To start the process, raise the beaker containing the gel and begin to pour the gel into an empty beaker beneath it. Once the gel starts to pour, turn the raised beaker upright again. The gel will move up the sides of the raised beaker as a thin film and then form thick strands as it falls into the lower beaker. This siphoning process can be repeated indefinitely by switching the raised and lowered beakers.

5. *(Optional)* Add a few crystals of a fluorescent dye such as fluorescein or rhodamine B to the alcohol before adding the polyethylene oxide. The gel can then be illuminated with a fluorescent lamp in a darkened room, creating a striking effect. Food coloring may also be used—add food dyes directly to the water in Step 2.

Polyethylene oxide has very low toxicity—it is actually used as a food additive. The high molecular weight of the polymer ensures that it is poorly absorbed in the gastrointestinal tract and will be completely and rapidly eliminated. The resin is neither a skin irritant nor a sensitizer, and it does not cause eye irritation either as the dry powder or in aqueous solution.

Demonstrations

Teacher Notes

Disposal

Consult your current *Flinn Scientific Catalog/Reference Manual* for general guidelines and specific procedures governing the disposal of laboratory waste. The polymer gel is 99% water and can be disposed of in the trash according to Flinn Suggested Disposal Method #26a.

Tips

- The alcohol acts as a dispersant to separate the polymer particles and inhibit the formation of large, insoluble lumps. Any water-soluble alcohol can be used as long as it is dry. In addition to methyl or ethyl alcohol, isopropyl alcohol, ethylene glycol, propylene glycol, and acetone may also be used as a dispersant.

- It is not necessary to use deionized or distilled water in this demonstration. The polyethylene oxide gel is nonionic and is not affected by the minerals in tap water.

Discussion

Polyethylene oxide is a nonionic, water-soluble, high molecular weight polymer. It is a polyether—every third atom in the polymer chain is an oxygen atom. The large number of oxygen atoms in the polymer chain leads to extensive hydrogen bonding with water molecules. The hydrogen bonding allows the polymer to dissolve in water despite its very high molecular weight (about 4,000,000).

The combination of being water soluble and having a high molecular weight gives polyethylene oxide many interesting properties and useful applications. Most unique is its ability to "thicken" water. The long polymer chains become intertwined like spaghetti and are heavily hydrogen-bonded to surrounding water molecules. The result is a "viscoelastic" gel. The high viscosity is due to the large number of hydrogen bonds between the polymer molecules and water, which create a molasses-like gel. The high elasticity is due to the ability of the very long polymer chains to straighten out when stretched and to slide past each other.

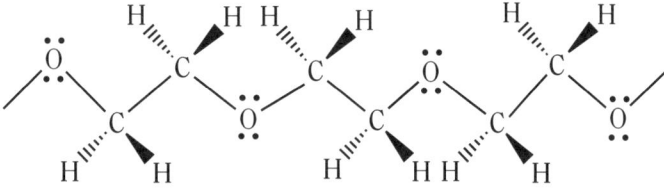

Figure 1. Structure of Polyethylene Oxide.

Polyethylene oxide is used to thicken and add a "soft and silky feel" to shampoos, hair conditioners, cold creams, and lotions. It is also used in inks, latex paints, cleaning solutions, and detergents.

Polyethylene oxide is a "straight-chain" polymer. Challenge your students to estimate the total length of a polyethylene oxide molecule having a molecular weight of 4,000,000.

To determine the length of the polymer chain, the length of the monomer repeating unit in polyethylene oxide must first be calculated. Answers will vary depending on the bond length and bond angle values used in the calculations. Some knowledge of geometry and trigonometry is required. The procedure on page 77 illustrates one possible approach to this problem.

Avoid getting the polymer gel on carpets or other fibers. It is almost impossible to wash out of materials. Rinse glassware with plenty of excess water.

Demonstrations

Teacher Notes

Length of the Monomer Repeating Unit

Average Bond Lengths: C—C 1.54 Å
(1 Å $= 10^{-10}$ m) C—O 1.43 Å

Estimated Bond Angles: C—C—O 112°
C—O—C 111°

Notice that the C—C—O and C—O—C bond angles deviate slightly from true tetrahedral bond angles (109.5°).

Repeating unit in polymer chain:

$$\text{Length of side } c = \sqrt{a^2 + b^2 - [2ab \cdot \cos \angle C]}$$

$$= \sqrt{(1.43 \text{ Å})^2 + (1.54 \text{ Å})^2 - [2(1.43 \text{ Å})(1.54 \text{ Å}) \cdot \cos 112°]}$$

$$= \sqrt{2.04 + 2.37 + 1.65}$$

$$= 2.46 \text{ Å}$$

Length of side x:

$$\frac{\sin A}{a} = \frac{\sin B}{b} = \frac{\sin C}{c}$$

$$\frac{\sin 90°}{1.43 \text{ Å}} = \frac{\sin (111°/2)}{x}$$

$$\frac{1}{1.43 \text{ Å}} = \frac{.82}{x}$$

side $x = 1.18$ Å

Length of monomer repeating unit = side c + side x = 2.46 Å + 1.18 Å = 3.64 Å

Length of a Polymer Chain

Polymer molecular weight = 4,000,000 g/mol

Monomer molecular weight = 44 g/mol

$$\frac{4{,}000{,}000 \text{ g/mol}}{44 \text{ g/mol}} = \approx 90{,}000 \text{ monomer units/polymer molecule}$$

(90,000 monomer units) (3.64 Å/unit) (1×10^{-10} m/Å) = 3×10^{-5} meters

Note: Results are rounded to one significant figure.

Special thanks to Walter Rohr, Eastchester High School, Eastchester NY, for supplying us with this activity.

Safety and Disposal

Safety and Disposal Guidelines

Safety Guidelines

Teachers owe their students a duty of care to protect them from harm and to take reasonable precautions to prevent accidents from occurring. A teacher's duty of care includes the following:

- Supervising students in the classroom.
- Providing adequate instructions for students to perform the tasks required of them.
- Warning students of the possible dangers involved in performing the activity.
- Providing safe facilities and equipment for the performance of the activity.
- Maintaining laboratory equipment in proper working order.

Safety Contract

The first step in creating a safe laboratory environment is to develop a safety contract that describes the rules of the laboratory for your students. Before a student ever sets foot in a laboratory, the safety contract should be reviewed and then signed by the student and a parent or guardian. Please contact Flinn Scientific at 800-452-1261 or visit the Flinn Website at www.flinnsci.com to request a free copy of the Flinn Scientific Safety Contract.

To fulfill your duty of care, observe the following guidelines:

1. **Be prepared.** Practice all experiments and demonstrations beforehand. Never perform a lab activity if you have not tested it, if you do not understand it, or if you do not have the resources to perform it safely.

2. **Set a good example.** The teacher is the most visible and important role model. Wear your safety goggles whenever you are working in the lab, even (or especially) when class is not in session. Students learn from your good example—whether you are preparing reagents, testing a procedure, or performing a demonstration.

3. **Maintain a safe lab environment.** Provide high-quality goggles that offer adequate protection and are comfortable to wear. Make sure there is proper safety equipment in the laboratory and that it is maintained in good working order. Inspect all safety equipment on a regular basis to ensure its readiness.

4. **Start with safety.** Incorporate safety into each laboratory exercise. Begin each lab period with a discussion of the properties of the chemicals or procedures used in the experiment and any special precautions—including goggle use—that must be observed. Pre-lab assignments are an ideal mechanism to ensure that students are prepared for lab and understand the safety precautions. Record all safety instruction in your lesson plan.

5. **Proper instruction.** Demonstrate new or unusual laboratory procedures before every activity. Instruct students on the safe way to handle chemicals, glassware, and equipment.

Safety and Disposal

6. **Supervision.** Never leave students unattended—always provide adequate supervision. Work with school administrators to make sure that class size does not exceed the capacity of the room or your ability to maintain a safe lab environment. Be prepared and alert to what students are doing so that you can prevent accidents before they happen.

7. **Understand your resources.** Know yourself, your students, and your resources. Use discretion in choosing experiments and demonstrations that match your background and fit within the knowledge and skill level of your students and the resources of your classroom. You are the best judge of what will work or not. Do not perform any activities that you feel are unsafe, that you are uncomfortable performing, or that you do not have the proper equipment for.

Safety Precautions

Specific safety precautions have been written for every experiment and demonstration in this book. The safety information describes the hazardous nature of each chemical and the specific precautions that must be followed to avoid exposure or accidents. The safety section also alerts you to potential dangers in the procedure or techniques. Regardless of what lab program you use, it is important to maintain a library of current Material Safety Data Sheets for all chemicals in your inventory. Please consult current MSDS for additional safety, handling, and disposal information.

Disposal Procedures

The disposal procedures included in this book are based on the Suggested Laboratory Chemical Disposal Procedures found in the *Flinn Scientific Catalog/Reference Manual*. The disposal procedures are only suggestions—do not use these procedures without first consulting with your local government regulatory officials.

Many of the experiments and demonstrations produce small volumes of aqueous solutions that can be flushed down the drain with excess water. Do not use this procedure if your drains empty into groundwater through a septic system or into a storm sewer. Local regulations may be more strict on drain disposal than the practices suggested in this book and in the *Flinn Scientific Catalog/Reference Manual*. You must determine what types of disposal procedures are permitted in your area—contact your local authorities.

Any suggested disposal method that includes "discard in the trash" requires your active attention and involvement. Make sure that the material is no longer reactive, is placed in a suitable container (plastic bag or bottle), and is in accordance with local landfill regulations. Please do not inadvertently perform any extra "demonstrations" due to unpredictable chemical reactions occurring in your trash can. Think before you throw!

Finally, please read all the narratives before you attempt any Suggested Laboratory Chemical Disposal Procedure found in your current *Flinn Scientific Catalog/Reference Manual*.

Flinn Scientific is your most trusted and reliable source of reference, safety, and disposal information for all chemicals used in the high school science lab. To request a complimentary copy of the most recent *Flinn Scientific Catalog/Reference Manual,* call us at 800-452-1261 or visit our Web site at www.flinnsci.com.

National Science Education Standards

Content Standards	Properties of Solids	Formula of an Ionic Compound	Lewis Structures and Molecular Geometry	The Color of Chemistry	Go Fish for an Ion	Electronegativity	Splatter Test	Graphite Disk Demonstration	Properties of Metals	Super Duper Polymer
Unifying Concepts and Processes										
Systems, order, and organization	✓		✓						✓	
Evidence, models, and explanation	✓	✓	✓	✓		✓	✓	✓	✓	
Constancy, change, and measurement		✓							✓	
Evolution and equilibrium		✓								
Form and function	✓			✓			✓		✓	✓
Science as Inquiry										
Identify questions and concepts that guide scientific investigation	✓	✓		✓						
Design and conduct scientific investigations	✓	✓	✓				✓	✓		
Use technology and mathematics to improve scientific investigations		✓								
Formulate and revise scientific explanations and models using logic and evidence	✓	✓		✓			✓	✓	✓	
Recognize and analyze alternative explanations and models										
Communicate and defend a scientific argument										
Understand scientific inquiry				✓						
Physical Science										
Structure of atoms										
Structure and properties of matter	✓	✓	✓	✓			✓	✓	✓	✓
Chemical reactions		✓		✓						
Motions and forces	✓	✓	✓	✓		✓	✓	✓	✓	✓
Conservation of energy and the increase in disorder									✓	
Interactions of energy and matter									✓	

Flinn ChemTopic™ Labs — Chemical Bonding

Content Standards *(continued)*

Experiments and Demonstrations

	Properties of Solids	Formula of an Ionic Compound	Lewis Structures and Molecular Geometry	The Color of Chemistry	Go Fish for an Ion	Electronegativity	Splatter Test	Graphite Disk Demonstration	Properties of Metals	Super Duper Polymer
Science and Technology										
Identify a problem or design an opportunity										
Propose designs and choose between alternative solutions										
Implement a proposed solution										
Evaluate the solution and its consequences										
Communicate the problem, process, and solution										
Understand science and technology										
Science in Personal and Social Perspectives										
Personal and community health										
Population growth										
Natural resources										
Environmental quality										
Natural and human-induced hazards										
Science and technology in local, national, and global challenges										
History and Nature of Science										
Science as a human endeavor				✓						
Nature of scientific knowledge										
Historical perspectives				✓						

Master Materials Guide

(for a class of 30 students working in pairs) **Experiments and Demonstrations**

Chemicals	Flinn Scientific Catalog No.	Properties of Solids	Formula of an Ionic Compound	Lewis Structures and Molecular Geometry	The Color of Chemistry	Go Fish for an Ion	Electronegativity	Splatter Test	Graphite Disk Demonstration	Properties of Metals	Super Duper Polymer
Acetone	A0009							5 mL			
Alizarin Red S	A0209				1 g						
Aluminum strips	A0178	1									
Aluminum shot	A0262	1 g									
Aluminum potassium sulfate	A0265				2 g						
Calcium oxide	C0263				1 g						
Candles	C0192	1									
Congo red	C0120				1 g						
Crystal violet	C0280				1 g						
Cupric chloride solution, 0.1 M	C0382		100 mL								
Ethyl alcohol	E0007							5 mL			
Food coloring	V0003										optional
Fluorescein	F0043										optional
Halite	AP4916	1									
Hexanes	H0046	100 mL							50 mL		
Indigo	I0057				2 g						
Iron nails	I0032	1									
Malachite green	M0129				1 g						
Methyl alcohol	M0054										25 mL
Methyl orange	M0076				2 g						
Quartz, agate	AP4930	1									
Sand	S0003	5 g									
Sodium carbonate	S0051				4 g						
Sodium chloride	S0061	5 g									
Sodium dithionite	S0446				6 g						
Sodium hydroxide solution, 3 M	S0447				6 mL						
Sodium phosphate tribasic solution, 0.1 M	S0250		100 mL								
Sodium sulfate	S0105				3 g						
Sodium sulfate decahydrate	S0225				6 g						
Stearic acid	S0356	5 g									
Sucrose	S0134	5 g									
Sulfuric acid, 18 M	S0228				1 mL						
Trichloroethylene	T0037								50 mL		

Continued on next page

Master Materials Guide

(for a class of 30 students working in pairs)

Experiments and Demonstrations

	Flinn Scientific Catalog No.	Properties of Solids	Formula of an Ionic Compound	Lewis Structures and Molecular Geometry	The Color of Chemistry	Go Fish for an Ion	Electronegativity	Splatter Test	Graphite Disk Demonstration	Properties of Metals	Super Duper Polymer
Glassware											
Beakers											
150-mL	GP1015	5									
400-mL	GP1025				14						
600-mL	GP1030										2
1-L	GP1040				7						
Graduated cylinders											
25-mL	GP2010										1
50-mL	GP2015								2		
Stirring rods	GP5075	15			10				1		1
Test tubes											
12 × 75 mm	GP6062		105								
13 × 100 mm	GP6063	75									
General Equipment and Miscellaneous											
Balance, centigram	OB2059	3									1
Bunsen burner	AP5344	15								1	
Ceramic fiber squares	AP1243									1	
Chenille wires	AP8862									1	
Conductivity meter	AP1493	5									
Crucible tongs	AP8266									1	
Evaporating dish, aluminum	AP6390	15									
Felt tip pen	AP1297		15		10						
Forceps, specimen	AB1093				30						
Go Fish for an Ion game	AP6131					1					
Hot plate	AP4674	5			7						
Inorganic/Organic Teacher Model Set	AP5455			1							
Metric ruler	AP4684		15								
Mortar and pestle	AP6066	5									
Multifiber test fabric	AP6135				2 m						
Ointment jar bottle with cap, 240-mL	AP8446								2		
Periodic table	AP9020			30							
Pipet, Beral-type, graduated	AP1721	30	30						3		
Reaction plate, 24-well	AP1447	15									

Continued on next page

Master Materials Guide

(for a class of 30 students working in pairs)

Experiments and Demonstrations

	Flinn Scientific Catalog No.	Properties of Solids	Formula of an Ionic Compound	Lewis Structures and Molecular Geometry	The Color of Chemistry	Go Fish for an Ion	Electronegativity	Splatter Test	Graphite Disk Demonstration	Properties of Metals	Super Duper Polymer
General Equipment and Miscellaneous, continued											
Scissors	AP5394			10						1	
Shapes of Molecules Model Set	AP5456		3								
Spatula	AP1323	15									
Styrofoam® balls, 1.5-inch	AP2280						4				
Styrofoam® balls, 2-inch	AP2281									25	
Super-Duper Polymer Gel	AP4556										4 g
Support stand	AP8226						2				
Test tube clamp	AP8217	15									
Test tube rack	AP5999	15	15								
Wash bottle	AP1668	15		30							
Water, distilled or deionized	W0007	✓		✓				✓	✓		
Weighing dishes	AP1279			70							
Wooden splints	AP4455	100									

Flinn ChemTopic™ Labs — Chemical Bonding